IN THE
SPIRIT
OF THE
GAME

IN THE
SPIRIT
OF THE
GAME

GOLF'S GREATEST STORIES

New York Times Best-selling Author

MATTHEW E. ADAMS

Author of *Fairways of Life*

THE LYONS PRESS
Guilford, Connecticut
An imprint of The Globe Pequot Presss

The Lyons Press is an imprint of The Globe Pequot Press.
The story "Buffalo Bill" was provided courtesy of Mark Cubbedge.

Interior images © Shutterstock.com
Text design by Jane Sheppard

Library of Congress Cataloging-in-Publication Data is available on file.
ISBN 978-1-59921-345-3

Printed in the United States of America
10 9 8 7 6 5 4 3 2 1

For my wife, Donna, and our sons, Austin and CJ.
Thank you for your love, patience, and inspiration.
You comprise my favorite partners in golf and in life.

OTHER BOOKS BY MATTHEW E. ADAMS

Chicken Soup for the Soul of America

Chicken Soup for the NASCAR Soul

Xtreme NASCAR Race Journal for Kids

Fast and Lean Racing Cookbook

Fairways of Life: Wisdom and Inspiration from the Greatest Game

Chicken Soup for the Woman Golfer's Soul

For more information, please log onto:
www.FairwaysofLife.com

CONTENTS

SPECIAL THANKS

George White

Mark Cubbedge

Mercer Baggs

AN INTRODUCTION TO
A PLACE OF MAGIC

It was early in the morning, barely past sunrise.

I needed to be at the golf course early because one of my members asked me to replace the shaft in his driver and said that he wanted to use it in the Saturday morning fourball.

"No problem," I told him. (I lied. It was a huge problem.)

Calling in favors, I asked my club fitter, Tommy Spargo, to do me a favor and install an NV shaft, 45 inches, tipped medium/firm.

"No problem, Matty," he obliged. "How soon do you need it?"

"Tomorrow," I replied, wincing on my end of the phone, waiting for his response.

After a momentary silence, which I likened to shock, Tommy let out a sigh and said, "Sure, buddy, no problem." (Obviously, he lied; it was a huge problem, but being the pro he is, he would get it done, just like he always does.)

"Thanks, Tommy. I owe you a pint of Guinness at the Twin Willows pub for this one," I limped into the phone.

"It'll cost a lot more than that . . ." his words trailed off as the next sound I heard was that of a dial tone.

With military precision, the club was ready as promised, and at 5:45 a.m., I was hopping from bridge to bridge, and island to island, across the Narragansett Bay to the Newport National Golf Club where I am proud to hold the position of general manager, in addition to my dabbling in golf television and literary pursuits. Hopping from my car, I handed the club to my eager member.

"Wow, I didn't think you would have it ready so fast," he opined.

"Of course," said I. "It was no problem at all," I lied, again.

Such is the life of those who toil in the trenches of the game. As much as things have changed since Walter Hagen and the pioneers of his era brought prestige and social respectability to the craft of those of us who work in the game, the basic essence of our job is still the same. Our job is to make your experience on the links as enjoyable as possible, whatever the cost.

I stood obediently and watched his foursome tee off, providing appropriate comments of encouragement and forbearing, as the individual instances called for. Happily on their way, the morning was mine.

"Now what are we going to do?" came a tiny voice from behind me.

Spinning, I saw my younger son, CJ, looking up at me with a mixture of lack-of-sleep-induced boredom and anticipation. In my march to duty, I had nearly forgotten that my six-year-old boy had soldiered to the golf course with me this morning.

"What would you like to do?" I replied in a classic deferring strategy, implored by parents across the millennia, who otherwise had no idea how to answer the charge.

"I would like to take a ride in a [golf] cart," came the simple request.

With that, we loaded into the electric cart-buggy and set out for the farthest regions of the course. Newport National is what I like to call a "modern links" course because it has all of the elements of a classic links course: hard turf, few trees, and heavy and ever-changing winds surrounding the island off Narragansett Bay, the Sakonnet Passage, and the Atlantic Ocean. What makes it "modern" is the fact that it stretches to over 7,244 yards. The course was designed by Arthur Hills and his associate Drew Rogers. I like to say that this former farm land and nursery were the canvas upon which Arthur and Drew crafted their masterpiece, but then, I know I am subject to flights of sentimentality. At the very, very least it is a brilliant golf course and a testament to building a championship-caliber golf course in harmony with environmental sensitivity and, in essence, only taking from the land that which it will give you. In that latter respect, I cannot think of an approach more in keeping with the ingenious designs of Donald Ross, whose work Arthur Hills's golf courses often remind me of.

As CJ and I rounded the path, to the eleventh hole, the dramatic sloping of the east side of the golf course opened itself to us. The ever present wind was stroking the hip-deep fescue as if it were a horse's mane, and the beams of sun breaking through cracks in the clouds lent an ethereal feel to the moment. All of this was framed by the deep blue horizon of the Atlantic Ocean. If I didn't know I was in Rhode Island, I would have sworn that I was in Waterville (Ireland). I don't know if I should be embarrassed, or if it should be celebrated in such a forum, but the profound beauty of the sight started to choke me up. I could barely speak.

"You know," I said to draw my lad's attention, "golf courses are places of magic," I muttered as I continued to motor down the crushed shell path.

CJ gave no reply. I wasn't sure if he even heard me. What's more, perhaps I never even said it aloud. Lost in my senseless emotion, I simply wasn't sure, either way.

Some two months later, I was called to the course on a similar early morning directive, and this time I had both CJ and his eight-year-old older brother, Austin, with me. After attending to the business of the day, the agenda belonged to my boys. It came as no shock that they wanted to go for a spin in the electric carts, and off we went.

As we wound our way around the golf course, which was still awakening from its cool and wet slumber, being appropriately trimmed and primed for the day's activities, we watched as rabbits and deer scurried across our path, more surprised at our presence than we were at theirs, I once again became lost in the sentimentality that often grips me on a golf course. So consumed was I in my immersed belief that golf courses are really God's gardens, that I almost missed a truly special moment, for a person of my sensibilities.

Thinking that I was lost in my misty observations, and therefore not monitoring their dialogue, my youngest son, CJ, turned to his older brother, intent to deliver an indisputable pearl.

"Golf courses are places of magic, you know," he said to Austin.

Austin paused, and then started to shake his head knowingly, finally replying simply, "I know."

I only made it another one hundred yards when I had to pull the cart over. "I need to inspect the depth of sand in this bunker," I proclaimed with authority. The real reason was that my eyes were too filled with tears to carry on. My boys, even at their tender ages, seemed to grasp that which distracts me to this day on every golf course upon which I set foot.

I often wonder if golf courses really are slices of heaven and that with death comes the *realization* that we were in heaven all along. I have heard golf described as religion, and if so, then golf courses are its cathedrals.

The game of golf has a way of revealing universal truths and aspects of our character that sometimes we would rather be left hidden, even from ourselves. It is a sport that is ever changing, challenging, and alive. Golf courses are more than manicured fields of sport, for they are portals in time and space. They bind us to that which came before us and will bridge us to that which will be after we are gone.

I wrote *In the Spirit of the Game: Golf's Greatest Stories* with the intent to capture and chronicle some of the stories and events that have helped shaped golf into the profound game that it is today. Stories from golf's heroes, from Old Tom Morris to Harry Vardon to Walter Hagen to Bobby Jones to Ben Hogan to Arnold Palmer to Jack Nicklaus to Tiger Woods, and many more in between, have been featured. While this is perhaps a noble cause, even my best efforts were doomed to failure before my pen ever married with paper. The depth of glory and significance and the characters from the game's history are too massive to chronicle in this anthology, and thus, I humbly and respectfully submit those that I did highlight as worthy entries in their own right. I hope that in future editions I can do justice to those stories that are screaming for an audience, but alas, the constraints of space and commerce only allowed for the enclosed in this edition, and it should not be interpreted that the stories featured here are any better than those that will be featured in future editions.

There was no science or ranking of worthiness that determined the stories and people I featured.

Much like life itself, golf is a game of triumph and tragedy. In the following pages, you may note that my focus was not to celebrate failure, shortcomings, or only harsh twists of fate, but rather to highlight the amazing accomplishments of those who rose above such constraints through cunning, skill, and determination.

My purpose for this effort is due to my fascination with history, and in particular, the history of the game. On a recent golfing holiday to Ireland with old friends, and through a Guinness-induced haze and the dim glow of a peat fire at a pub just outside the town of Lahinch, my dear friend Danny McLaughlin revealed a belief that he had apparently been harboring for many years.

Turning his red face to mine, he declared, "I think you were born one hundred years too late."

"I beg your pardon?" said I.

He continued without repeating, fully aware that I had heard every word and that my reply was simply a plea to clarify the statement, "Because of your love and respect for history. You treat it as something more than just what happened in the past, you celebrate it; you glorify it. I mean, you are the only guy I know that gets excited over a pile of rocks" (for the record, the rocks in question were not just "*a pile of rocks*," it was the site of an ancient castle).

Not knowing exactly how to respond, I took a long, slow drink from my pint in an attempt to buy time to think, which undoubtedly left me with a beer-foam mustache. I was somewhat stunned by the comment, but not in the manner of offense. Rather, I felt the way you feel when someone peers into your soul and pulls out a nugget of truth so undeniable that you simply nod in understanding and conformance. For to me, I do not view the time in which we live with any particular conceit. I do not feel that the era we exist in is any better than any era that preceded it. I do not use terms to define our time such as a "modern era" for to use such words is only to provide folly for the generations that will follow us and laugh at our self-importance. Nor rather, do I look upon the past with pity, for I do not think they peered forward with lament for things such as air conditioning or motor cars any more so than you and I lament that our cars do not drive themselves or that we are not capable of moving from place to place by molecular displacement. In its essence, I believe people are people and regardless of where, or when, you existed on this earth, we all felt the same emotions: love, concern for our families, companionship, the desire for accomplishment, and the need to compete.

To me, there can be no better a forum for such a celebration of life than on the timeless stretch of land defined by a golf course, for the struggle of the human condition that is played out there, in all of its drama. As a longtime co-author for the *Chicken Soup for the Soul* series and as illustrated in my 2006 book, *Fairways of Life—Wisdom and Inspiration from the Greatest Game*, I believe the greatest champions are those who face any endeavor with a plan and the knowledge that adversity is not something simply to avoid, for its arrival is inevitable. Rather, it should be met with expectation and a conviction to overcome its inherent obstacles through tenacity, focus, hard work, and a game plan. Maintaining a proper, posi-tive perspective and a sense of humor are the arma-ments to carry with you into the battle. While all of this is presented in the context of the sport of golf, I actually think that these universal lessons hold true whether the fairways you walk in your life are cov-ered with grass, marble, wood, or cement.

In the end, I did not attempt this literary effort to be a simple recounting of the events that have defined the game, as worthy as that calling may be, but rather, I hoped that this book would be a historical anthol-ogy to support my theory that golf courses truly are places of magic.

Enjoy.

—Matthew E. Adams
April 2008

IN THE
SPIRIT
OF THE
GAME

"I think you have to really, really want to do it before it's going to happen."
—David Toms

CHAPTER ONE

RISING TO THE OCCASION

A CROWNING MOMENT

Arnold Palmer's prowess at the Masters Tournament is well chronicled with four of his career total seven Majors coming from Augusta. The tournament, in many ways, embodied him, leading columnist Johnny Hendrix of the *Augusta Chronicle* to coin the phrase, "Arnie's Army" to define his fiercely loyal legions of fans who were very much a part of the legend.

At the 1960 Masters, Palmer personified his image with birdies on the last two holes to once again edge Ken Venturi by a margin of one stroke. After his 1958 victory, it was his second green jacket.

Notwithstanding Palmer's Masters dominance, the individual tournament that may best epitomize his golfing legend in its entirety—his go-for-broke, fearless style of attacking a golf course—was displayed in all of its raging glory at the 1960 U.S. Open at Cherry Hills, outside of Denver, Colorado.

Palmer came into the tournament with his confidence at an all-time high. Not only was he the reigning Masters champion, but he had also won four other tournaments that year. It seemed that whenever he teed it up, he was in contention, and Cherry Hills was a course that fit his eye.

However, through three rounds of the tournament, Palmer uncharacteristically found himself mired in fifteenth place, seven shots behind the leader, Mike Souchak.

It seemed that Palmer just could not get it going, as the events on the very first hole of the tournament seemed to be a premonition of mediocrity for him at this U.S. Open. Attempting to drive the first green, a 346-yard par 4, he pushed his tee shot into a ditch and, after a penalty drop, posted a tournament-opening double bogey six. Ironic, that his attempt to drive the first green would prove so costly as the same hole, same shot, would play such a dramatic role come Saturday afternoon (U.S. Opens were played with thirty-six holes on Saturday in those days). Undaunted by the results of the first round, Palmer would attempt to drive the green in the second and third rounds as well, missing the mark on both occasions.

"Success in golf depends less on strength of body than upon strength of mind and character."

—Arnold Palmer

On Saturday, between the morning and afternoon rounds, Palmer sat eating a cheeseburger and drinking iced tea with Ken Venturi, Bob Rosburg, and writers Bob Drum and Dan Jenkins.

According to several sources, the conversation at the table went something like this:

"I might shoot 65," said Palmer. "What would that do?"

"Nothing," harrumphed Drum. "You're too far back."

"It would give me 280. Doesn't 280 always win the [U.S.] Open?" Palmer reasoned.

"Yeah," chuckled Drum. "When Hogan shoots it."

With that, an angry Palmer marched from the table.

Standing on the first tee, Palmer faced the same decision he had faced in three previous rounds. Should he go for the green or play it safe? Anyone who knows anything about Arnold Palmer knows that there was little debate. The fact that he was seven shots back only furthered his resolve. This time, his persimmon driver delivered a crushing blow that sent the ball rocketing on a perfect trajectory. Bouncing through a belt of rough before the green, the ball slowed just enough for it to settle on the green, some 20 feet from the hole (Palmer would later say that he was so fired up that if his ball had not been slowed by the rough, he feared it would have ended up over the green). His eagle putt barely crept past the edge of the hole, settling some 2 feet past. Palmer would convert the birdie putt.

At the second hole, he would miss the green with his second shot but secure a birdie nonetheless with a chip-in. A close wedge shot at the third would nail down another birdie, and a 20-foot putt on the fourth hole would give him yet another. At this point, he was two under and had cut Souchak's lead to three shots.

Surprisingly, Palmer would only par the short, par-5 fifth hole, after greenside bunkering his second shot with a 3-wood. However, on the sixth hole, a 7-iron would put him back on the birdie train, and another birdie at the seventh would equate to six birdies in seven holes.

"Put him three strokes behind anybody, and he believes he's the favorite."

—Frank Beard on the competitive mentality of Arnold Palmer

He would hit a bump at the eighth hole with a bogey, after hooking his 2-iron into a bunker at the 230-yard, uphill par 3. He would adequately extract himself from the bunker to 3 feet from the hole, but he missed the putt.

Palmer would par the ninth hole to finish the front nine in an incredible score of 30 and jam himself right back into contention.

In a glimpse of things to come, while Palmer was completing his front side, a twenty-year-old amateur named Jack Nicklaus, who was paired with Ben Hogan, held the tournament lead at 5 under par. Nicklaus was one ahead of Palmer and a host of other contenders, including Hogan, Julius Boros, Dow Finsterwald, Jack Fleck, who started out with birdies on five of the first six holes (he beat Hogan at the U.S. Open in 1955), and Don Cherry, one of golf's great but often forgotten characters who was an accomplished nightclub singer in the style of Sinatra and who was clearly capable of making beautiful music on the golf course as well. As amazing as Palmer's front nine score of 30 was, the young Nicklaus cruised through nine with a highly respectable 32.

It is easy to record the score, comment on its brilliance, and then assume that Palmer simply tore through the competition with the same magnitude that he did the golf course in that final round. However, the performance of Nicklaus and the gritty determination of the forty-seven-year-old Hogan provided insight that a whole host of significant contenders were ready to duke out this tournament down the stretch. As is normally the case in a U.S. Open, it would come down to who had better control of their nerves.

"What other people may find in poetry or art museums, I find in the flight of a good drive."
—Arnold Palmer

Nicklaus made a costly error on the thirteenth hole. With 3 feet left to save par and maintain a one-stroke lead in the tournament, Nicklaus noticed a poorly repaired ball mark in his path. It can be speculated that the young amateur, in awe and perhaps slightly intimidated by the reputation of the legend, Hogan, with whom he was paired, failed to ask the great champion if he agreed the mark needed further tending. Deciding instead to putt through it, the mini-crater redirected the ball's path just enough to spin it out of the hole, resulting in a bogey. He would follow by three-putting the fourteenth hole.

One by one, the leaders would start to fall away as pressure and nerves compounded errors and blurred precise decision making.

Palmer, however, continued to march onward. He would post another birdie at the par-5 eleventh hole and then post pars on holes twelve through sixteen. At this point, the only golfer standing between him and the U.S. Open Championship was none other than Ben Hogan. Playing two groups in front of

IN THE SPIRIT OF THE GAME

Palmer, Hogan had hit thirty-four of thirty-four greens through the day's play. As was the case with him in his waning years on Tour, it was the putter that had kept Hogan from absolutely running away with this tournament, as his play from tee to green was still unmatched. At the 555-yard, par-5 seventeenth hole, Hogan reasoned that he needed to make birdie if he was to stay in the thick of it. Expertly leaving his second shot positioned before water that fronted the green, Hogan decided to play a delicate pitch shot in front of a front-cut pin. If such a risky strategy was a reflection of not wanting to put too much pressure on his shaky putter, it could be well reasoned, but the effort came up 6 inches too short, and his ball agonizingly dribbled back down a fronting mound and into the edge of the water. From there, having removed his shoes and socks, he would place the ball on the green and two-putt for bogey. Hogan now faced the urgent prospect of needing a birdie on the final hole if he was to have any chance. The eighteenth is defined by the same body of water that played such a role on the last hole, and eager to maximize his chances for birdie with a short iron to the green, Hogan's line was too aggressive on the drive, and his ball plunged into the water, some will attest, only inches from safety. Instead of a birdie, he would post a 7, finishing the tournament in ninth place.

Inasmuch as one would think that Hogan, after going 4 over par on the last two holes, would be consumed by his own lament, he stated, "I played thirty-six holes today with a kid who should have won this thing by ten strokes." An apt premonition of things to come.

Having witnessed Hogan's demise, Palmer employed a conservative strategy and cruised home with the Championship in hand, finishing two strokes in front of second place, Jack Nicklaus.

The significance of three of the greatest golfers of all time converging in this Major was not lost on those chronicling the game at that time. *Sports Illustrated*'s Dan Jenkins wrote that "on that afternoon in the span of just eighteen holes, we witnessed the arrival of Nicklaus, the coronation of Palmer, and the end of Hogan."

The victory was a massive boost to Palmer's surging dominance and popularity. Having secured the first two legs of the modern Grand Slam, he looked to that summer's Centennial Open Championship at St Andrews, hoping to continue his march to immortality. His march, however, would come up one shot short, as he came in second to Kel Nagle (nearly coming back from being seven strokes down after thirty-six holes). Ironically, he would finish seven shots back at the PGA Championship.

While the 1960 U.S. Open would be Palmer's only U.S. Open title, his score of 65 set a Championship record, and his comeback from being seven shots back set a record that still stands to this day. In addition, his sole victory in this event should not be seen as a reflection of having difficulty with the tournament's setup. On the contrary, between 1959 and 1975, he was in the top five on ten occasions and in the top-ten thirteen times, including four second-place finishes.

Arnold Palmer's days of dominance are remembered for many things, including the Masters, his resurgence at The Open Championship (what Americans call "the British Open"), carrying the game to unprecedented heights of popularity, and, at the 1960 U.S. Open, driving the first green and, in so doing, searing his legend.

SHOT OF A LIFETIME

What if your entire career was remembered for one climactic moment?

Such was the case for the legendary Gene Sarazen, author of one of the most famous shots in Masters history, a double eagle on the par-5 fifteenth hole (rivaled in drama, timing, and impact by Tiger Woods's chip-in for birdie at the sixteenth hole in 2005).

The feat took place in 1935, and it is said to have put the Masters on the map of the world sports stage. While this perspective has its merits, it also deserves to be viewed in an appropriate historical perspective.

Nineteen thirty-five was the second year of the event. Sarazen had missed the inaugural tournament due to a commitment to play in a series of exhibitions in

South Africa with Joe Kirkwood, an infamous trick-shot artist (and another true, classic character of the era). While today a golfer would be criticized if he passed up an invitation to the Masters to play in an exhibition, in 1934 the tournament was known simply as the "Augusta National Invitational Tournament" and would not be known by its more famous moniker for another few years. It was, however, the personal party of the sport's reigning icon, Bobby Jones, and a disappointed Sarazen made it a point to ensure he was there in 1935.

Sarazen started the 1935 tournament with a solid 68, one stroke behind first-round leader Henry Picard, and he followed that with a 71. Rain arrived for the third round, and Sarazen shot a 73. Therefore, heading into the final round, he stood at 4 under par, a total of 212, and in fourth place, three shots behind the leader, Craig Wood.

In an era before modern pairing considerations (such as television), Wood actually teed off four groups in front of Sarazen, who was paired with Walter Hagen.

Wood would post a 3-over-par score of 39 going out, which gave hope to the pursuers chasing him. Taking advantage, Sarazen started strong and at one point was tied for the lead before bogies on the ninth and tenth holes dropped him back. Wood, who had finished second in the prior year's inaugural tournament, had steadied himself, picking up two strokes to par on the back side, through the seventeenth hole. At this time, Hagen and Sarazen were at the tee box of the reachable, par-5, 485-yard fifteenth hole with Sarazen trailing Wood by two strokes. The fairway before him sloped from right to left, and Sarazen launched a long drive that used the hole's contour to his advantage. His drive settled near the crest of the hill some 235 yards from the green.

"I don't care what you say about me. Just spell the name right."

—Gene Sarazen

As Hagen and Sarazen reached their drives, they heard a roar from the eighteenth green echoing through the pines. They assumed, and soon it was confirmed, that Wood had birdied the eighteenth and Sarazen's deficit now stood at three strokes. Upon hearing the news, Hagen is reported to have said, "Well, that's that," and he played his second shot safely before the water fronting the green. Years later, Sarazen speculated that Hagen's posture at that moment was not an admission of defeat, as the forty-two-year-old legend was not a threat to catch Wood (Hagen would finish tied for fifteenth place, at 5 over par), but was intended to send a message to Sarazen to hurry up and play a safe shot to keep things moving as Hagen reportedly had a special date waiting for him to finish.

Sarazen surveyed his options and decided that going for the green was his only option if he was to shave three strokes to par over the final four holes to catch Wood.

His ball lay behind a small crest in the hill in a slight depression. Deciding that he needed loft, he chose his new Wilson 4-wood, which featured a scalloped back. Although the term did not exist then, the club was arguably the game's first "hybrid" club (which is remarkable in light of the credit Sarazen is already given for his part in the development of the modern sand wedge). Before hitting the shot, Sarazen rubbed his good-luck ring on the forehead of his caddie, "Stovepipe," for luck. The ring was given to him by a friend who claimed it once belonged to Mexican president Benito Juarez, who was supposed to have been wearing the ring on the night he was elected (this account is widely disputed). Sarazen was renowned as a fast player, and he took little time over the shot. Toeing the club to decrease its loft, he lashed at the ball with a swing that distinguished him as a power golfer, despite his 5-foot 4-inch frame.

In 1935 the green complex was not as it is today with less banking and a smaller body of water fronting the green. Sarazen's ball narrowly cleared the water, bounced onto the putting surface, then rolled from right to left directly toward the pin, before diving into the hole. Contrary to popular belief, there were only a couple dozen patrons surrounding the green at the time. Significantly, Bobby Jones numbered among them as he had made his way down from the clubhouse to watch his friends finish (Jones, who had finished well before, had rounds of 74, 72, 73, and 78 to finish tied for twenty-fifth). Sarazen would later note that one of the most satisfying things about making the shot was the fact that it was witnessed by both Jones and Hagen.

When word of what had happened got back to the clubhouse, it was met with shocked disbelief. Members of the media had been congratulating Wood, and the name on the winner's check (of $1,500) had reportedly already been drawn out to Wood. Sarazen's deficit-erasing score caused an additional conundrum for the media in that they did not know what to call the accomplishment of three under par on one hole, eventually convening and deciding upon the name "double eagle" over other suggestions such as "a twin dodo."

As history tends to skip pages, it is important to note that Sarazen still had work ahead of him after the double eagle if he was to maintain his share of the lead. He posted scores of par on the sixteenth and seventeenth holes. At the uphill eighteenth hole, he struck an uncharacteristically weak drive that resulted in him calling upon the services of his heroic 4-wood once again to reach the green. Two putts later and he had earned his place in a playoff.

"The difference between winning and losing is always a mental one."

—Peter Thomson

The next day, Sarazen and Wood squared off in a thirty-six-hole playoff, the only one in the tournament's history. As it appeared that fate was already on Sarazen's side, the results of the playoff would prove to be a testament to the same, as he soundly defeated Wood, 144 (71–73) to 149 (75–74), to win by five shots. It is interesting to note that the two times Sarazen played the fifteenth hole in the playoff, he would post only pars on the site of such drama only a day earlier.

The victory would mark Sarazen as the first man to accomplish the career professional Grand Slam with victories in the (British) Open Championship, the U.S. Open, the PGA Championship, and the Masters. Of course, this distinction was not noted for many years later, as the "Augusta National Invitational Tournament" was not looked on as a "Major" at that time, and the concept of the Grand Slam being something other than what Bobby Jones had accomplished five years earlier did not take shape until the dominating years of Ben Hogan.

Nonetheless, Sarazen's spectacular shot not only defined his career but also helped lay down a Major foundation.

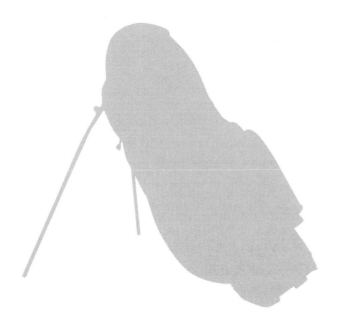

A SHOCKING RECORD

Coming into the 1973 U.S. Open at Oakmont, the sense of a daunting challenge was palatable. Oakmont was well used to its starring role on the nation's most prominent national stage, and it carried with it more than just the pedigree of having hosted four national championships. As the site of Hogan's last U.S. Open victory in 1953 and Nicklaus's first, in 1962 (in a play-off over Arnold Palmer), the course also carried with it a reputation for sporting America's fastest greens and fairways that were so narrow that even the USGA had to ask the membership to *widen* two fairways in preparation for the National Championship.

The course, while only modestly longer (27 yards) than it had been for its last Open in 1962, had bunkers that were legendary, if not only for their unique variety but also, for this Open, their pure quantity, at

187, an increase of 33. What's more, the seventeenth hole, a previously short par 4 (292 yards), which Hogan had driven in 1953 and Palmer in 1962, had been lengthened to 322 yards, and the fairway contoured from right to left to bring bunkers into play for an overly aggressive line.

The story lines for this Open centered on the game's reigning icon, Jack Nicklaus. He would be attempting to win his fourth U.S. Open, tying him with his hero, Bobby Jones, for U.S. Open titles but surpassing him in total "Majors" won at fourteen (Jones's Majors included U.S. and British Amateurs, in keeping with the mentality from the era in which he competed). In addition, as any western Pennsylvania golf fan would easily recall, Nicklaus's victory in 1962 came at the hands of their own, Palmer, and in 1973, at the age of forty-three, the great man still possessed enough of a game to claim revenge.

While the weather for the opening round was perfect for playing the game of golf, the golf course had awakened that morning in a spiteful mood. Having dried out somewhat from rain earlier in the week, the course was starting to run. In order to score at Oakmont, the ball must be played to the proper spot on its large and undulating greens, all the harder to do when finite ball control is difficult to achieve. To the shock of nearly everyone, 1965 Champion Gary Player would finish the day having posted an impressive 67, some three shots clear of his closest pursuers, Jim Colbert, Ray Floyd, and Lee Trevino. Player's mark was the lowest single round for a U.S. Open at Oakmont up until that time. What made Player's 4-under-par performance all the more remarkable was the fact that due to his February bladder surgery, Player had played in only three tournaments over the preceding five months!

In every great story, some element of mystery always seems to find its place. Such was the case on the Thursday night after the first round. It has been stated that the intention of the tournament committee and the grounds crew had been to water the thirsty greens only for five minutes, just enough to give them a sip of satisfaction but not enough to change their cruel disposition. For reasons that have remained unclear, the water was not turned off after five minutes, and the greens, by Oakmont standards, became like sponges. Most likely caused by simple human error, the effect on the second round of the tournament was dramatic as the players attacked the defenseless lamb-greens like a pack of wolves.

A club professional from East Norwich, Long Island, named Gene Borek, who got in as an alternate when Dave Hill withdrew, sent an early message about the changing fortunes of the course when he fired a new course record 65 in the morning. Whereas the day before, only four men broke par, more than four times that number would post red numbers on Day 2. It is interesting, then, that Gary Player, who had excelled in the difficult conditions a day earlier, would muster only a 1-under-par performance in the second round. However, he would still hold the thirty-six-hole lead at 5 under par, one stroke ahead of Colbert. Nicklaus was three shots off the lead, and Palmer was five shots back. Palmer continued to electrify the crowd, identically matching pars for birdies with eight each through the first two rounds.

"The U.S. Open is the hardest Major to win."
—Johnny Miller

If tournament officials had hoped that Mother Nature would help rescue them from their green miscue, they were sadly mistaken. Saturday morning brought with it a storm that dropped heavy rain on the course, but the skies cleared up enough by 10:20 a.m. for the first starting time to tee off on schedule. The rain would continue to come back, off and on, throughout the rest of the day, continuing the trend from the day before and causing the greens to lose a strong element of their defense. The inevitable rust in Gary Player's game was finally forced from the shadows on Day 3 in conditions that would lend one to believe it should have been the opposite: He shot a 6-over-par 77. By the end of the day, Arnold Palmer would own a share of the lead with 1952 and 1963 U.S. Open Champion Julius Boros, who was fifty-three years old (and already the oldest man to win a Major championship when he won the 1968 PGA Cham-pionship at age forty-eight), Jerry Heard, and John Schlee. Tom Weiskopf, who would win The Open Championship (British) one month later, was one stroke behind.

With Palmer tied for the lead, the level of excitement for the final round had reached a fevered pitch. Everyone expected Arnold Palmer to come out firing at every pin; the volatile mixture of this being the area where he was from, the sense of the event owing him something from '62, and the reality that Palmer was not getting younger and this could be one of his last chances to contend were all ingredients of the gumbo. What's more, no one expected Jack Nicklaus to roll over; to the contrary, the golf world awoke that Sunday morning expecting nothing less than another epic battle. What the golf world got was perhaps the greatest final round of a Major of all time.

Two-time PGA Tour winner Johnny Miller awoke on Sunday morning six shots from the leaders and separated by twelve hungry men. While he had posted eight top-ten finishes so far that season, he had not had a victory, and his most recent U.S. Open performance hardly gave him reason to be confident. One year earlier, at the final round of the U.S. Open at Pebble Beach (won by Nicklaus), Miller shot a disappointing 79 to finish seventh.

He informed his wife to be packed and ready to go immediately following his final round because after a 5-over-par 76 the day before, a day when the rest of the leaders were moving the other direction, he was merely managing his expectations.

This was despite some very strange happenings throughout the tournament. All week, Miller was followed by a woman claiming to be a psychic and "knowing" that he would win the U.S. Open that week. In his locker before the final round, Miller claims he found a letter postmarked from Iowa that simply said, "You are going to win the U.S. Open." No name, no return address.

"Serenity is knowing that your worst shot is still pretty good."
—Johnny Miller

On the practice tee, Miller claimed that an unrelenting "voice" within him was urging him to open his stance, even beyond that employed by Lee Trevino. It was a compulsion that he would acquiesce to.

Miller would start the final round one hour ahead of the leaders. A 5-iron set up birdie on the first hole, a nearly jarred 9-iron on the second, and another 5-iron on the third hole (and 25-foot putt). Quickly, he was 3 under on the day. It didn't stop there. He made birdie from the greenside bunker at the par-5 fourth hole, and all of a sudden, standing now at 1 under par, the thought of winning this golf tournament did not seem so foreign to him.

A sense of reality set in during the middle of his front nine with pars on the fifth, sixth, and seventh holes. He three-putted the eighth hole for bogey and dropped to 3 under for the day and even par for the Championship. A birdie on the short, par-5 ninth hole would get him back on track.

He would par the tenth hole, then wedge his approach to 15 feet at the eleventh hole for another birdie to move to 5 under for the day, 2 under for the tournament, and within striking distance of the lead.

About this time, the leaders were finishing up their front nine in what was a hectic and frenzied final round. Veterans Palmer and Boros continued to fight the good fight, and through nine, they held a share of the lead with Tom Weiskopf, with Lee Trevino among the players only a stroke back. As there seems to be a modern perception that players tend to fall off the pace on the final day of Majors, the first nine holes of this U.S. Open was proving to be a slugfest.

Some measure of adversity would strike Miller at the 603-yard, par-5 twelfth hole. His drive would find the rough, and the most club he could get on the ball was a 7-iron from this lie. He would now need to hit a 4-iron to reach the putting surface. Miller would stick it to within 15 feet and convert the putt. He now stood at 6 under for the day and 3 under for the tournament.

Word of Miller's historic pace began to filter through the course, and in an attempt to catch history in the making, the gallery started to surge across the footbridge that spanned the Pennsylvania Turnpike to catch a glimpse. So determined were the frenzied legions that some even crawled across the foot-wide railing as traffic zoomed past beneath them.

Miller's 4-iron proved to be an asset again on the thirteenth hole when he used it to laser his approach to 5 feet and convert yet another birdie. Now, he stood at 7 under for the day and 4 under for the tournament, tied for the lead with Palmer.

He left his birdie putt on the fourteenth hole an inch from dropping, thus setting up the fifteenth hole for appropriate drama. This hole was a 453-yard par 4 that was not only intimidating for its length in 1973 but also for its 34-yard-wide fairway and bunkers on each side. Playing as if fate had found its hero, Miller hit his drive some 275 yards and stuck his trusty 4-iron shot to within 10 feet of the pin. His birdie putt split the hole and with it, he owned sole possession of the lead at 5 under par for the Championship and 8 under for the day's round.

"Golf is a matter of confidence. If you think you cannot do it, there is no chance you will."
—Henry Cotton

Behind him, Palmer's fortunes began to unravel on the eleventh hole. Sitting only four feet from the hole to go to 5 under for the tournament, Palmer would miss the putt. After what looked like a perfect drive on the twelfth hole, he would be shocked to find his ball had kicked into heavy rough, and he would end up bogeying the hole, followed by bogies on holes thirteen and fourteen.

Miller would par the par-3 sixteenth hole with a 3-wood and two putts; he would also par the par-4 seventeenth hole utilizing a 1-iron, wedge, and two putts, and then on the par-4 eighteenth hole, Miller unleashed a huge drive (and final exclamation point), leaving him only a 7-iron to get home, and two putts later (his birdie putt would spin out of the hole), he would post a score of 63, the lowest ever in a U.S. Open (it would be matched by Nicklaus and Weiskopf in 1980 at Baltusrol).

Now forced to wait out the players still on the course, Miller knew his fate was no longer in his hands. In a gritty performance, Schlee had crawled his way back to within one stroke of Miller and would need a birdie on the eighteenth hole to tie. Schlee's approach shot rolled through the green into a patch of difficult rough some 40 feet from the pin. With Miller closely watching, Schlee was unable to coax the ball to the hole and he tapped in for par, finishing with an even par, 71. Now, only Tom Weiskopf (who missed a short putt on the seventeenth hole) could catch Miller, and he would have to jar his second shot at eighteen to do it. When the unlikely failed to happen, Johnny Miller had won his first U.S. Open.

Miller would finish the day with a 32 on the front, a 31 on the back side, and having hit every green in regulation.

When it was all done, Schlee finished in second place, Weiskopf in third, and Palmer, Trevino, and Nicklaus tied for fourth.

ONE FOR THE AGES— THE MIRACLE OF '86

There really wasn't much reason for optimism. Jack Nicklaus, after all, was forty-six years old. And this was the Masters. Jack hadn't won a tournament in two years, hadn't won a Major in six years. It had been nine years since he had played as many as sixteen tournaments in one year.

So there really was no reason to think that in 1986 Jack Nicklaus would be able to do what everyone considered "impossible." He was, in his own words, "an old guy out there playing golf who wasn't supposed to compete anymore."

Jack himself could understand the public's general perception. It had been "five years," he said, since he really, truly cared about being a touring professional golfer. By the time he was forty-six, he was heavily into his course design business, he was getting into the golf club business, and he had a number of outside interests to occupy his time. He was the proud father of five grown children and had a very active life. In short, he wasn't Jack Nicklaus who was totally into competing at golf. He was now Jack Nicklaus, the man who was more into family and business than he was at winning golf tournaments. He had his time, and it was brilliant by any account.

"I really wasn't working at it that hard," admitted Jack. "Did I try to prepare? Sure. But I didn't prepare to the extent that I did when I was right in the middle. I just didn't have any motivation to move in that direction."

It was against that backdrop that Nicklaus went to Augusta in '86. With him for the first time ever in his professional career was his mother. And he did care greatly about Augusta, where he had won five times. He loved the course and the club overall, and this was one tournament that he prepared for like no other.

"Resolve never to quit, never to give up, no matter what the situation."
—Jack Nicklaus

In playing seven tournaments leading into Augusta in '86, Nicklaus had missed the cut three times, withdrew from another event, and didn't have a finish higher than thirty-ninth.

The late Tom McCollister was a golf writer in Atlanta at the time, and a friend of Nicklaus. He had handicapped the field early in the week, giving his choices for the eventual winner. His opinion of Jack's chances, however, wasn't good. He cast Jack as a 100-to-1 shot, saying his pal was "washed up."

A friend of Nicklaus spotted the story and taped it to the refrigerator in the house in which Jack was staying. It was in a very prominent position, front and center on the refrigerator door. Every time Jack went to the fridge, he was certain to have a look at the article. It was, Nicklaus admitted, "a little extra motivation."

What wasn't generally known that year, by McCollister or anyone else, was that Jack actually had putted very well early that year. He had stumbled onto a large-faced putter, one the press immediately dubbed the "omelet pan." The putter was destined to become famous by Sunday night.

"I hadn't really hit the ball that well, I hadn't really done very much golf-wise," he said. "I don't know, I'd won a grand total of a couple thousand dollars or something, maybe a couple hundred dollars. I don't even know what I'd won, but anyway it wasn't very much.

"And I got to Augusta and I started hitting the ball better. Augusta always sort of inspired me. I always went in the week before. I always prepared myself and always got ready for the golf tournament, and I did the same thing that I normally do to try to get ready. I enjoyed that—it was always fun for me to do so."

The tournament began and Nicklaus didn't do much. He shot 74, which was six shots worse than the leaders. McCollister's prediction appeared to be coming true. No one, it seemed, cared what Jack might or might not accomplish the remainder of the week.

Thursday evening, Nicklaus was depressed because, "I played pretty well but I didn't make any putts, I didn't putt very well." He found reason for optimism, however, because his putting hadn't been a problem all spring—the problem had been his ball-striking. And now his ball-striking was pure. If he could find his putting touch again, then there was at least some hope for the last three rounds.

And sure enough, Jack went out Friday and shot a 71, then followed that on Saturday with a 69. He still wasn't anyone's choice to add a sixth green jacket, not with Seve Ballesteros, Greg Norman, Nick Faldo, Tom Kite, Tom Watson, and Bernhard Langer in the field, and all looking like potential champions. But Nicklaus was getting a little attention now because this forty-six-year-old man was looking like he might have a chance to finish in the top ten. He had climbed all the way to the eighth position, just four shots out of the lead.

Sunday morning Jack received a call from his son Steve. In the course of conversation, Steve asked, "What do you think it will take, Pops?"

"I think 65 will win the tournament," said Nicklaus. "I think 66 will put me in a playoff." Son Steve said, "Exact number I had in mind. Just go shoot it."

Jack didn't do much to shoot a 65 the first eight holes. He had a bogey and a birdie and was even par for the day. On number nine, though, he was preparing to putt a 12-footer for birdie when he heard a big roar from number eight, then almost immediately heard another from the same area, then another as the players had all hit magnificent shots. Jack turned to his playing partner, Sandy Lyle, and with a grin said, "Hey, why don't we see if we can make a little noise ourselves?"

Then he poured in the putt, the first of several as he set out on his famous march to another green jacket.

"Ask yourself how many shots you would have saved if you never lost your temper, never got down on yourself, always developed a strategy before you hit, and always played within your capabilities."

—Jack Nicklaus

"Not that it made any difference at that point because I was still 10 miles behind," said Nicklaus. "But I holed a 25-footer at the next hole [number ten] and a 25-footer at the next hole [number eleven]. And I said, 'That's pretty exciting. Now I'm nervous.' You know, why would I be nervous? I mean I'm not even anywhere near it, but I'm nervous because I think I can get into contention."

Jack woke up to reality a bit at number twelve, the short par 3, when he missed a 6-foot par putt and made bogey. But wonder of wonders, that bogey might have eventually meant the championship. "It might have—it put me back—brought me back to the reality that, you know, that I have got to still play golf," said Nicklaus.

Number thirteen is a par 5, and with a good drive and 3-iron, he hit the green in two shots and made another birdie—his fourth in five holes. Jack parred fourteen, but on the par-5 fifteenth it was time for yet another series of heroic shots.

"I hit a really nice drive—put it in the right position on the fairway," he remembered. "And I turned to

Jackie [his son Jack Jr. was his caddie that day] and I said, 'How far do you think a 3 will go here?'"

Nicklaus meant a 3 on the scorecard. He had glanced over the leaderboard, where Kite, Norman, Ballesteros, and Watson were battling furiously to squeeze out an advantage. And Jackie knew exactly what Nicklaus meant.

"He said, 'I think it will go a long way, Pops.'

"So I just took dead aim on it and it never left the pin. And then it started to trickle down to the left about 12 feet." He had covered the 240-yard distance with a 4-iron, his adrenaline was riding so high. And then he strode up to the ball, bent over in his famous crouching stance, and stroked it into the cup for an eagle.

Could it be? Well, could it? At last, Nicklaus knew that he was right in the heart of contention.

"Now I'm pumped," Nicklaus said. "I know I'm just a couple of shots behind at that point."

Now came sixteen, and this wasn't Jack Nicklaus, occasional golfer and full-time businessman. This was Jack Nicklaus circa 1964, when his whole focus was what happened on the golf course. And at sixteen, he swung a 5-iron from 175 yards and heard Jackie say, "Be right." The reply from Jack: "It is.

"It was one of those times where I hit the shot and as soon as it left the club, I knew exactly where it was," he said. "It was just sort of a cocky remark that I made. I don't normally make that. But I had so much confidence in what was going on, that's what I did."

The ball landed 12 feet from the hole. Jack studied the putt closely.

"You know, it is not as easy a putt as it looked because I had a little putt that was sort of—it wasn't dead straight forward, it was a little putt that would break backward in front of the green. So I had to take it inside the left edge. And I made the putt, obviously, and the place went wild."

So Nicklaus walked to the seventeenth and heard another huge rumble from the crowd. Ballesteros, playing at the fifteenth, had knocked his approach into the water. Seve took a bogey, and suddenly Nicklaus had the lead—though at the time he didn't realize it.

Jack half-wanted to cry, half-wanted to shout. "I saw [Ballesteros] out in the fairway and I knew he'd hit it in the water," said Nicklaus. "And I hate that sound because half of the sound is half of the cheering for me, which I don't like when somebody makes

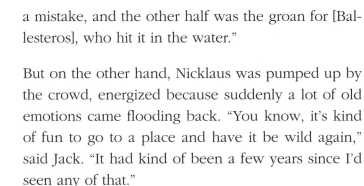

a mistake, and the other half was the groan for [Ballesteros], who hit it in the water."

But on the other hand, Nicklaus was pumped up by the crowd, energized because suddenly a lot of old emotions came flooding back. "You know, it's kind of fun to go to a place and have it be wild again," said Jack. "It had kind of been a few years since I'd seen any of that."

A drive and a wedge from 110 yards put him just 12 feet from the flag at the seventeenth. "I looked at Jackie and he said, 'Dad, it's got to go right,'" recalled Nicklaus Senior. "I said, 'I know it's going to go right, Jack,' but I said, 'I think it's going to come back left at the hole.'"

The putt did exactly as he thought—for yet another bird. Now Nicklaus knew exactly where he stood, knew he had the lead by himself. Up ahead of him was the final hole, and a perfect drive left him 175 yards to the flag.

Unfortunately, just as he swung his 5-iron, he felt a gust of wind hit him in the face, and he knew that wasn't good news. The ball dropped 40 feet below the pin. But here Jack had another secret weapon—intimate local knowledge of the green, since his architectural company had redone this green during the summer of '85.

He knew the putt would be faster than it once was, but it wouldn't have the extreme break of years past. He stroked it with these thoughts in his mind, and it was a perfect lag putt. One more tap-in, and Nicklaus had completed the back nine in 30 strokes for a final round 65. Sixty-five, exactly the number he had predicted to Steve in the morning phone call.

Nicklaus had done all he could. Now there was a matter of a forty-five-minute wait in the Jones Cabin while Norman and Kite each had chances to tie him.

The best chance came from Norman, who had made four consecutive birdies beginning at the fourteenth hole. As he played the eighteenth hole, he had tied Jack for the lead. Norman hit his approach from the middle of the fairway, a 4-iron, but alas, he blocked it into the crowd. He could only make bogey, and forty-six-year-old Jack Nicklaus was the champion.

It was quite possibly his most-watched win ever, with television cameras joining the live crowd, which was trumpeting his every move for two and a half hours. And even today, Jack admits he gets tingles when he watches the old film of the Miracle of '86.

"It was just the end of a great week," he says. "It was not only fun, but it was something really neat to think that, you know, here I've come back. And I hadn't worked out. I'd been playing twelve tournaments a year, going through the motions.

"It was kind of a neat week, a neat thing to go through. It was great for me because it felt like I actually had done something well."

Jack Nicklaus's final ledger shows seventy-three PGA Tour victories, eighteen professional majors, ten Champions Tour wins, and eleven international victories. But never, never did Jack win as meaningful a title as the 1986 Masters.

CHAPTER TWO

FROM THE BEGINNING

> *"You are not to remove stones, bones or any break club for the sake of playing your ball, except upon the fair green, and that only within a club's length of the ball."*
>
> —From the Original Rules of Golf, 1744

BAN GOLF!

It will come as no great surprise that the Scots and the English have had a long and sometimes contemptuous relationship. What may come as a bit of a surprise is how this complicated union had a significant impact on the development of the game of golf.

Feeling the need to constantly train their forces, particularly in archery, it was, so to speak, a burr in the saddle of King James II of Scotland that his able-bodied men would choose to invest their time in less purposeful pursuits like golf. So, in 1457 he banned the playing of the game, along with football (soccer), opting to force his subjects to engage in activities that would hopefully result in the protection of his kingdom, rather than wasting time with something as trivial as golf. Perhaps the king's time would have been better spent on the golf course, as the golf gods apparently got the last word. As an ardent supporter of the mechanized arms of the day, the king bolstered his forces with massive and powerful cannons to be used to reduce the castle walls of his enemies to rubble. The golf-ban-making king met his demise soon after his golf ban, as he made the mistake of stationing himself too close to one of his cannons during yet another battle against the enemies of the Crown. The art of loading a cannon with gunpowder, lighting it, and using its explosive power to blast a projectile in the direction of your enemies is a gamey proposition to say the least. Well, for King James II, this reality hit home, quite literally. You see, the cannon misfired, blowing itself to bits along with King James II. Nonetheless, King James's successors apparently saw the wisdom of his golf ban (notwithstanding the risk of earning the wrath of the golf gods), as it continued to be reiterated and upheld by both his son and grandson (although it is widely believed that the kings still secretly played), until such time as its practicality could not stand in the way of the game that is very much a part of the Scottish identity. In 1502 King James IV signed the Treaty of Glasgow, intended to ensure everlasting peace with England (which, ultimately, it didn't). He also clearly possessed a practical romanticism, as he married Margaret Tudor, daughter of Henry VI, the man who signed the treaty on England's behalf. Apparently he was secure in the fact that a lasting peace had been achieved, because it is interesting to note that it was King James IV himself who was one of the first to take to the links, on March 29, 1506, in a match against the Earl of Bothwell, perhaps contributing to the game's Scottish lineage as a "royal" game. Their match took place on royal hunting grounds that are now the home to the Sterling Golf Club. No record was kept for who won the match, but my money is on the king.

Perhaps most interesting of all is the fact that the Scottish ban on golf has never officially been lifted.

THE FIRST GOLF WIDOW

Over the years, much has been said about the lament of the lonely wife who waits at home while her golf-obsessed husband feeds his golfing addiction. The moniker (often self-applied) for this source of festering resentment is a "golf widow."

However, history shows us that the first "golf widow" was not left behind; rather, she was the queen of the house, literally.

Mary Queen of Scots was born in 1542, the child of King James V and Mary of Guise. Merely a week after her birth, Mary's father died, making her an infant queen. Mary was sent away to France to be formally educated while her mother served as regent.

Mary Queen of Scots possessed an impressive lineage. Through her grandmother, Margaret Tudor, sister to King Henry VIII, she also had a claim to the English Crown, and, through her mother, ties with one of France's most powerful families, The House of Guise.

While in France, Mary played and fell in love with the game of golf. It is speculated that it was this very bond that ultimately led to her tragic demise.

At the age of fifteen, Mary, who was raised as a Catholic, married Francis II, son of Henri II of France and Catherine Medici of the powerful Medici family of Italy. However, the union was over two years later with the death of Francis, resulting in Mary losing any claim to the French Crown. So, in 1560 (after the death of her mother), Mary returned to Scotland to claim her rightful position.

Mary brought her love of the game back to Scotland as well. Reported to suffer from a recurrent slice, the 6-foot-tall Mary often traveled with a huge party of attendants while on the links. Due to her French rearing, most of her closest attendants were called by the French word "cadet." It is speculated that the native Scots had difficulty pronouncing this word and, thus, the word "caddie" was introduced into the game of golf for the first time.

Mary's second husband, Lord Darnley, was murdered. Within days of her husband's sad demise, there was Mary, out slicing the ball around the links. Her failure to properly mourn her husband's death caused an uproar and fueled speculation that she had conspired with James Hepburn, the fourth Earl of Bothwell, to remove her husband; it also raised some sticky claims of accession to the throne. Mary did not help her cause when she married James Hepburn within months of the murder.

Matters grew from bad to worse as her third marriage (to the earl) put her in conflict with other Scottish nobles whose support she desperately needed. Ultimately, the political firestorm was too much, and she abdicated the throne to her son, James VI of Scotland (who later became James I of England). She fled to England seeking asylum.

Mary's cousin, Queen Elizabeth, was not ready to trigger a war over her arrival and put Mary under house arrest for the next eighteen years. Mary would eventually be accused of engaging in treasonous activities and sentenced to death by the axe.

Apparently, her axe-man suffered from the same inefficient slice as Mary, as it took him three attempts to slice off her head.

THE TEST OF TIME

Imagine, for a moment, that Father Time has a face.

The image is a stolid one, unaffected by joy or grief, pleasure or pain. From his face, lined by experience, flows a beard grayed with wisdom, dignity, respect, joy, and sorrow.

Pan down his body and there, at his side, flows a chain that connects, inevitably, to a watch.

Now take this legendary keeper of the years and place him in St Andrews, Scotland. That face you see belongs to Old Tom Morris, legendary keeper of the green.

No sport venerates its past more profoundly than the royal and ancient game, and Tom Morris Sr. is chief among its iconic characters.

Morris's life has only been transcended by his death, where, a century after his passing, time has transformed "The Grand Old Man of Golf" into a mythical figure whose image invokes the very spirit of the game.

Old Tom, as he is fondly known, spans the gap from Allan Robertson, golf's first professional, and Willie Park Sr., its first (British) Open champion, to The Great Triumvirate of Harry Vardon, James Braid, and J.H. Taylor—and today remains in the very fiber of the game, somehow untouched by the passing of time.

Morris, despite being age thirty-nine when he helped found The Open, played in every tournament beginning with the inaugural one in 1860 up through 1896, when he was seventy-five.

Morris won The Open four times—in 1861, 1862, 1864, and 1867—the latter of which came at age forty-six years, ninety-nine days—a record that remains unchallenged today.

His 1862 victory also has weathered the ages. That thirteen-stroke victory remains the benchmark of domination in golf's oldest championship.

Morris got his start at St Andrews when Robertson hired him as an apprentice to work in his shop, thus changing Morris's plans of becoming a carpenter. It was there, while working in St Andrews for Robertson, that Morris honed his abilities as a club maker, feather-ball maker, and, of course, as a player.

Morris's working relationship with Robertson began to deteriorate when Morris took up using the new gutta percha ball—an invention Robertson frowned upon because it was in direct competition with his livelihood of making featheries.

Their falling-out eventually saw Morris accept an invitation from Col. James Fairlie (whom Morris would later name a son after) to become the keeper of the green at Prestwick in 1851. Prestwick, the birthplace of The Open, would play host to the first twelve events and see Morris win three of the first five tournaments.

Morris returned to St Andrews as both professional and keeper of the green in 1864—a position he held until his death in 1908. Morris was unquestionably St Andrews' foremost resident, setting up a shop adjacent to The Old Course's eighteenth green, where he made clubs, appeared at tournaments, and, as St Andrews entrenched itself as golf's home, became its patriarchal figure.

Golf truly ran in Morris's blood. He fathered three sons, two of whom were successful golfers—James Fairlie Morris and Tommy Morris (better known as Young Tom). Young Tom competed in his first professional event when he was only thirteen, winning an exhibition match in Perth and claiming the £15 first prize.

Young Tom's proficiency with a set of golf clubs is why it can be said no man not named Morris ever won an Open championship by double digits. Young Tom won four successive Opens and furthered the family's golfing prowess as the best of the day.

His first Open title came in 1868 and made him the youngest winner at age seventeen. He also made the first ace in Open history that year. In 1869 and 1870 he won by eleven and twelve strokes, respectively. The latter of those margins included a round of 47, which is considered the first great round of golf. Remember in those days tournaments consisted of three rounds of twelve holes, so by way of comparison today, and in order to put this considerable achievement into perspective, think for a moment about a golfer distancing himself from the field by twelve strokes after two rounds.

Young Tom followed that round of 47 with a pair of 51s, giving him a 149 total and breaking the tournament record by five shots. His 149 would stand through the remainder of the thirty-six-hole days of The Open (1892) and, perhaps even more astounding, the thirty-six-hole record would hold through 1908—well into the rubber-ball era.

In the book *Golf's Greatest*, it was written that Young Tom "was simply too good for the available competition."

By winning The (British) Open in three successive years (1868–1870), Morris permanently won the Challenge Belt, the tournament's first prize, as the rules of the competition stated anyone who won three years in succession won the belt outright.

His excellence in the tournament necessitated the creation of the most recognizable trophy in golf—the Claret Jug—which he also became the first to win when the tournament returned in 1872.

What Young Tom enjoyed in quality he, sadly, lacked in quantity. While it is true Young Tom completely altered his contemporaries' belief of how well the game could be played—he was a powerful ball striker, master of the recovery from poor lies, revolutionary with his iron play, and robotically consistent with his putting—his time in the game was tragically short.

In September of 1875 Young Tom's wife passed away during childbirth while delivering a stillborn baby. Three months later, on Christmas Day, Young Tom himself died at age twenty-four—often reported as dying from a broken heart but correctly credited as succumbing to a lung hemorrhage.

Indeed Old Tom had to endure the death of a grandson, daughter-in-law, and son in three months' time. He would eventually have to bear the death of all three of his sons, a fate he handled with similar dignity and class as he did playing golf.

Old Tom was characterized by one of the day's most notable writers, John L. Low, as "always cheerful during a life which met with almost continual disappointments and sorrows." No one less than Horace Hutchinson said that Old Tom was a beacon of humbleness.

In Hutchinson's *The Book of Golf and Golfers,* he wrote that Morris "has been written of as often as a Prime Minister, he has been photographed as often as professional beauty, and yet he remains, through all the advertisement, exactly the same, simple and kindly."

Old Tom's contributions as an architect remain as vivid as his presence in the game. During his life it is estimated he laid out or helped sculpt between sixty and seventy-five courses, including Carnoustie, Prestwick, Westward Ho!, Royal Dornoch, St Andrews, and Lahinch. His impact in this field influenced many of the most prominent designers known today, including C. B. Macdonald, Alister MacKenzie, A. W. Tillinghast, Harry Colt, and Donald Ross.

Old Tom passed away at age eighty-seven in 1908, and those turning out to pay their respects lined the entire length of South Street in St Andrews and caused Andrew Kirkaldy to remark, "There were many wet eyes among us for Old Tom was beloved by everybody."

In 1983 the Golf Course Superintendents Association of America began presenting the Old Tom Morris award, which is presented to an individual who, through a continuing lifetime commitment to the game of golf, has helped to mold the welfare of the game in a manner and style exemplified by Old Tom Morris.

Proving Old Tom's place in the game remains indelible, the Royal Bank of Scotland issued a special £5

note in 2004 commemorating the 250th anniversary of The Royal and Ancient Golf Club of St Andrews. The note featured the likeness of Old Tom Morris.

Perhaps Old Tom's place in the game is best memorialized by the most famous finishing hole in golf—the eighteenth hole at The Old Course in St Andrews. For it is this hole that was named in his honor.

Like the game whose image he reflects, Old Tom has certainly stood the test of time.

CHAPTER THREE

PERSONALITIES
AND CHARACTERS

*"To be a champion,
you must act
like one."*
—Henry Cotton

A GRIP ON STARDOM

Legends like Harry Vardon surely are born bearing
the mark of greatness, are they not? To realize their
potential, all it will take is the merging of circumstance and opportunity to see their latent talents
bloom and fate fulfilled. Or so it would seem. For
as certain as one can be about Vardon's legendary
status, his attainment of such a position was as much
about conviction as ability.

The word "legend" carries with it an element of something wonderful and amazing, even mystical, something that the ordinary man is seemingly lacking.

Famed early-twentieth-century golf writer Bernard Darwin thought he knew what "it" was that Vardon possessed and most others did not. "I do not think anyone who saw him play in his prime will disagree to this, that a greater genius is inconceivable," wrote Darwin, the first man to cover golf on a daily basis with such a particular expertise and the expression of a poet.

Fortunately for Vardon, genius cares not for wealth or status. It simply attaches itself to one it deems worthy.

For his career, Vardon won six Open Championship titles—still unmatched today—and one U.S. Open, the first Englishman to do so. He was a golf architect, an author, and the driving force behind the popular grip that bears his name and that many of today's golfers still use. Trophies are handed out by the PGA of America and European Tour in his honor. He was among the first group of inductees into the World Golf Hall of Fame in 1974.

Yes, Vardon may well have been a great golfing genius, for he did showcase an incredible amount of capacity and aptitude for the game. That he was a professional golfer at all is a testament to his considerable skills and desire. Born May 9, 1870, in Grouville, Jersey—one of the Channel Islands between England and France—Vardon was raised in a very modest environment, hardly the privileged upbringing that was considered a must for such a profession. It was something he would forever have to battle, a class system that told him even despite his future accomplishments, he was not worthy of standing shoulder to shoulder with the highest ranks of English society.

He first played the game using crude, handmade clubs fashioned from oak. He would bat a marble ball, called a taw, around a course measuring about 50 yards.

Young Harry, one of eight Vardon children, didn't spend much time as a child playing rounds of golf. Rather, he furthered his golfing education by serving as a caddie. It wasn't until the age of twenty that Harry began to make a living off the sport. In 1890, at the behest of his older brother, Tom, he left his Jersey home to take the position of Green Keeper and Professional at Studley Royal Golf Club in Yorkshire.

A former employer for whom Vardon used to caddie once advised Harry, "Never give up the sport. It might prove useful in the future." Curious as to his abilities, and inspired by such words of encouragement, Vardon became competitive on a professional level.

"Don't play too much golf," Harry is famous for saying. "Two rounds a day is plenty."

In addition to his genius, Vardon had a genuine love for the game. He also possessed the most fluid and repetitive swing of his generation. Vardon, standing 5 feet 9 inches and weighing 155 pounds, had an upright stance. He hit his ball high and landed it softly on the greens. And while most everyone else was trying to manipulate a primitive ball with inconsistent hickory clubs, Vardon was monotonous, in the greatest sense of the word. Monotony led to efficiency, which in turn led to winning and then winning some more.

Perhaps most impressive regarding Vardon's fluidity was the seeming rigidity of his dress. Vardon was the first professional to play in knickers. He also donned a hard-collared shirt, tie, and buttoned jacket. And yet there was freedom in his swing among this cumbersome attire.

In 1896 Vardon captured his first Open Championship title, doing so at Muirfield, Scotland. He beat J. H. Taylor in a playoff. It was not the first and would certainly not be the last time that the two butted heads on a golf course.

Together, Vardon and Taylor were a part of the "Great Triumvirate." Of course, triumvirate indicates three, and the third man among these golfing greats was James Braid.

This trio represented the leading British golfers in the late nineteenth and early twentieth centuries. Taylor and Braid, much like Vardon, were men of modest origins. Men who refused to let societal norms and public opinion dictate the course of their lives.

Vardon, Taylor, and Braid defined their era. They were the bridge between Old and Young Tom Morris and Bobby Jones and Gene Sarazen.

From Taylor's triumph in 1894 to Vardon's victory in 1914, the Triumvirate accounted for sixteen Open Championship crowns in twenty-one years. Entering the 1914 edition at Prestwick, Scotland, the three men were tied with five Open titles apiece. Vardon would separate himself from the pack by beating Taylor by three.

That would be the final Major win for the three men. The Open was not contested from 1915–1919 due to the first Great War. One can only imagine how many more Majors Vardon would have won had life not intervened, or had it actually been convenient for him to travel back and forth from Britain and America, or had there actually been a PGA Championship or Masters Tournament before 1916.

Nonetheless, Vardon spent as much time in the United States as he could. In fact, he became as well known in the United States as he was in the United Kingdom, golf's first global star.

As is the case still today with many of the European-born stars, the lure of fame and finance brought Vardon west across the Atlantic to compete in America. He did so in 1900—beating who else but Taylor by two strokes at Chicago Golf Club—to become the first Englishman to win both the British and U.S. Opens.

Vardon made his money and, to many, his name by competing in exhibition matches in the United States. He played more than eighty of them in 1900 alone, winning more than seventy times, often doing so against the better-ball of two opponents. Vardon, with his reputation and resume, was a man men loved to challenge—and a man most men could not beat.

In 1903 Vardon became severely ill, so much so that he was taken to Mundesley Sanatorium in Norfolk. There, he was diagnosed with tuberculosis. Vardon survived, but his health was permanently affected.

Amazingly, he managed to win The Open for a fourth time that same year. He earned No. 5 in 1911 and, of course, No. 6 three years thereafter.

The 1914 Open Championship was Vardon's last Major title, though he did come close to winning the 1920 U.S. Open. Vardon, at the age of fifty, led by four shots with seven holes to play until Mother Nature and a balky putter conspired to relegate him to second place.

Just because you're a legend doesn't mean you're always a winner. For some, Vardon will be most remembered for a Major championship in which he did not win.

In 1913 Vardon and fellow Brit Edward "Ted" Ray lost the U.S. Open in a playoff to Francis Ouimet at The Country Club in Brookline, Massachusetts. Ouimet was a local amateur, a twenty-year-old unknown caddie. A kid from a working-class family, unwelcomed at the doormat of the financially fortunate. A child who was simply captivated and enraptured by the game. Someone to whom Vardon, whether he knew it or not at the time, could relate.

"To play well you must feel tranquil and at peace. I have never been troubled by nerves in golf because I felt I had nothing to lose and everything to gain."

—Harry Vardon

That match has been called "The Greatest Game Ever." It's been memorialized in print and on the silver screen.

Ouimet's win helped popularize golf in America. His shocking defeat of the great Harry Vardon was the catalyst the game needed on this side of the Atlantic.

Vardon was the perfect foil for Ouimet. He wasn't just golf's first great international player; he was the game's first international celebrity. He had his own ball named after him, the AG Spalding "Vardon Flyer." He endorsed muscle balm and health tonics and golf coats. He commanded Tiger Woods–like (for the times) appearance fees.

Vardon's playing career began to wind down in the mid-1920s. He competed in his final Open Championship in 1926. Eleven years later, on March 20, he passed away. To this day, members of South Herts Golf Club, where Vardon was club professional from 1903 until his death, lay a wreath at his burial site. They then play for the Harry Vardon Trophy. His famed overlapping grip is the club's emblem.

Golf, from its beginnings, has been believed to be for the wealthy. A game for kings and aristocrats. A noble sport not for the common man.

But golf, as Harry Vardon showed, is an open sport. Open to those who slap around a marble ball with a stick and a conviction that greatness is not only for those who are privileged.

THE BABE

The stories, the accolades, the achievements in a life otherwise cut short are almost beyond comprehension. Mildred "Babe" Ella Didrikson Zaharias (as an adult, she would change the spelling of her last name from *Didriksen* to *Didrikson* to reflect the Norwegian spelling, rather than the Swedish) could well be the most consummate athlete ever to grace the fairways. She was labeled with the nickname "Babe" after hitting five home runs in a single baseball game as a youth.

The daughter of Norwegian immigrants, she was born in Port Arthur, Texas, in 1911. According to several accounts, including her own writing, Babe liked to claim that she was born in 1914, but both her birth certificate and gravestone claim the earlier date. What cannot be disputed is that she was one of those rarely gifted athletes who seemed to excel at every sport she tried, which included, basketball, baseball, softball, track and field, diving, football, roller-skating, bowling, and even boxing, but it would be golf that would most secure her lasting legend.

In 1930 her first job was that of a secretary for the Employers Casualty Insurance Company of Dallas, Texas. While it is claimed that she even excelled at typing (capable of typing eighty-six words per minute on the old typewriters that favored a powerful, downward strike), it appears that the position was simply a conduit to play on one of the Industrial League basketball teams, under the authority of the AAU. She would lead her squad to the AAU Basketball Championship in 1931. Representing her company at the 1932 AAU Championships, she competed in eight events, winning five of them—shot put, baseball throw, long jump, javelin, and the 80m hurdles—tying for first in the high jump and setting five world records in a single day. On the strength of her performance, her team garnered thirty points to beat the next closest team by eight points. However, unlike her competition, she was the only person on her team!

Her performance at the AAU Championships qualified her for the 1932 Olympics in Los Angeles. Limited to competing in three events, she won gold medals in the 80m hurdles and the javelin throw, setting world records in both, and the silver medal in the high jump. She would have won gold in the high jump event as well, but her unorthodox (for the time) style of jumping head first was too much for the judges, and they declared her the silver medalist. Later that year, she was named the Woman Athlete of the Year by the Associated Press (she would also win this honor in 1945, 1946, 1947, 1950, and 1954, a total of six times). In 1950 she was named the AP's Woman Athlete of the First Half of the Twentieth Century.

She played baseball for the touring baseball team, the House of David, and once pitched an inning in an exhibition baseball game where she struck out Joe DiMaggio.

In the early 1930s she turned to the sport of golf, a game she was not exposed to while growing up in Texas. However, her natural athleticism soon took over, and in short order she was redefining the meaning of being a woman golfer. Up until her arrival on the scene, women's golf was defined by elegant apparel and gracious, if not powerful, swings.

Babe Didrikson would smash that stereotype with her awesomely powerful swings, which have been visually compared to those of Lee Trevino in his prime.

She would explain her lack of constraint when lashing into the ball, "It's not enough just to swing at the ball. You've got to loosen your girdle and really let the ball have it."

"Luck? Sure. But only after long practice and only with the ability to think under pressure."
—Babe Didrikson Zaharias

She more than let the ball have it, she redefined the sport. In 1938 she competed in the Los Angeles Open, the only woman to compete in a men's tournament for the next six decades. At that tournament, she would meet George Zaharias, a professional wrestler and

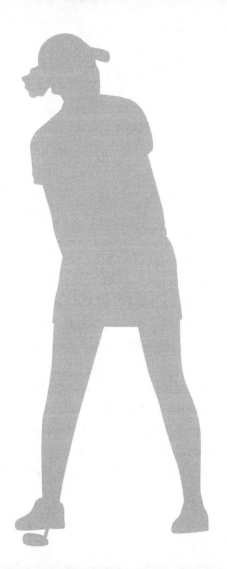

sports promoter. They would marry eleven months later and live in Tampa, Florida.

Zaharias may have been late to come to the game of golf, but she quickly made up for lost time. At one time she won seventeen straight amateur tournaments in a row. She was the 1946 and 1947 United States Women's Amateur Champion and was the first American to win the British Ladies Amateur Championship, also in 1947. She was one of thirteen founding members of the LPGA. To this day, she holds the LPGA records for being the fastest golfer to ten wins (one year and twenty days), twenty wins (two years and four months), and thirty wins (five years and twenty-two days). While competing, she served as the president of the LPGA from 1952 to 1955. In 1950 she won the women's version of the Grand Slam holding the three women's Majors of the day, the U.S. Open, the Titleholders Championship, and the Western Open. She won ten Major champion-

ships (U.S. Open 1948, 1950, and 1954; Titleholders 1947, 1950, and 1952; Western Open 1940, 1944, 1945, and 1950) and a total of forty-one professional tournaments.

"The formula for success is simple; practice and concentration, then more practice and concentration."

—Babe Didrikson Zaharias

Zaharias was diagnosed with colon cancer in 1953. She made a comeback in 1954, winning the U.S. Open only a month after surgery and the Vare Trophy for the lowest scoring average. Her cancer would flare up again in 1955, and she was limited to playing in only eight events (winning two of them). The cancer continued to progress and finally took her life in 1956, at age forty-five.

While too brief, the impact she made on the sport was formidable. In 1954 she received the Richardson Award by the Golf Writers Association of America for her contributions to golf and the Ben Hogan Award for her comeback after the cancer surgeries. She was awarded the USGA Bobby Jones Award in 1957 and named the *Sports Illustrated* Individual Female Athlete of the Century in 1999. That same year, the Associated Press named her the Top Woman Athlete of the Century, and she was named in the Top 10 on the list of the 50 Greatest North American Athletes of the past 100 years for ESPN's SportsCentury, the only female to make the Top 10. In 2000 she was recognized as one of the LPGA's Top 50 Players. She was one of six original inductees to the LPGA Hall of Fame in 1967. She was named to the Hall of Fame of Women's Golf in 1951 and is enshrined in the World Golf Hall of Fame.

TO BE A PLAYER

Young Gary Player had to be out of the house by 6:00 a.m. in order to catch the first of two different buses that would take turns bouncing him—along Johannesburg's unimproved roadways—the better part of 30 miles to the King Edward VII School.

When he returned home at day's end, darkness was there to welcome the child back to the cold bench in front of the quiet and empty house, where Gary would wait for his father, Harry, to return from work in the gold mine.

Gary's mother, Muriel, had recently passed away from cancer, and his oldest sibling, Ian, was away in Italy serving during World War II. Wilma, Gary's sister and five years his elder, had taken a job to help relieve the family's financial stress.

To this day Gary has no recollection of ever sitting on that bench and feeling sorry for himself.

Undoubtedly those early experiences add perspective to one of Gary's more profound sayings today: "There is no success without effort. There is no reward without work. Some people think life owes them something: wealth, respect, or peace of mind. I don't mind telling you that this attitude makes me sick."

The fact that hard work and hard times were unavoidable parts of life was instilled in Gary at a very early age. Both Harry and Ian drilled into him that meeting the challenges of life began with positive thinking and was followed up with a steady diet of hard work and dedicated effort.

"Nonsense," Harry replied when a teenaged Gary suggested his diminutive size would keep him from becoming a champion, "it all depends on the guts you have. It's what's inside of you that matters, not what's on the outside."

When Gary was just seven years old, he learned one of his first valuable life lessons from Ian. Outside the family house was a grapevine of which Gary was very protective. One afternoon he saw several neighborhood boys in the tree and demanded they come down. They did, and one of the bigger boys grabbed a handful of grapes and smeared them right in his face.

Gary ran crying to Ian, relaying the story and expecting a sympathetic ear. Instead, Ian sat him down firmly and told him he couldn't run from his problems in life. He had to face them head on.

Ian proceeded to string a rope some 35 feet in the air on one of the highest branches in the yard. He told Gary to climb the rope every day to build his muscles and strength. Ian also taught Gary to box and put him on a weightlifting and workout regimen—a religious routine for Gary today that finds him in better shape than men one-third his age.

"We create success or failure on the course primarily by our thoughts."
—Gary Player

As much as Harry and Ian were "indefatigable disciplinarians," these guiding figures in Gary's life were equally nourishing and encouraging. It was Ian who whittled Gary's first golf club, while Harry, a

2-handicapper, first took Gary to a golf course. Much to everyone's surprise, Gary made par on three consecutive holes, and the wheels for what would become the career of one of the game's greatest global champions were set in motion.

Gary turned pro in 1953 at age eighteen. Outside of himself, his family, and a few close friends, few gave him much of a chance of success. Local sportswriters said he would never make it big. Money was tight so Harry took out a loan to finance Gary's first year on the South African Tour. Gary pitched in by playing with used golf balls to save on expenses. His clothes were shabby, he remembers, but they were also the best he had.

Two years after turning pro, Gary won his first event on the South African Tour, the 1955 East Rand Open. The congratulations that followed from other players and tournament officials were swallowed by one particular gesture. Harry approached his son and extended his hand for a man-to-man handshake. The pride Gary saw in his father's eyes remains one of the most moving experiences of his life. At that point Gary felt as if he had become a man.

Later that year Gary was able to travel to foreign soil to compete for the first time. The members at Killarney Golf Club in Johannesburg, where Gary was the assistant pro, took up a collection of what amounted to $500. That money, coupled with an overdraft arranged by his father at the bank, sent Gary on the road for what they figured to be two months.

Gary's first stop was Cairo for the Egyptian Match Play Championship, which he eventually won over another South African, Harold Henning. His winnings, then a rich $900, were pinched to the max—including lugging all his own bags from station to train and train to station to avoid having to tip. His miserly ways extended his trip an additional three months as he played the British golf circuit.

In 1956 a twenty-year-old Gary Player set a handful of lofty career goals for himself. Among them was his desire to win The Open Championship, the Masters, the PGA Championship, and the U.S. Open. At the time, the professional Career Grand Slam had been won by only two individuals, Gene Sarazen and Ben Hogan. Amazingly, Player would achieve this lifetime goal before he reached his thirtieth birthday.

Each of those four crucial steps weren't without their own lessons, all of which reinforced what his father and brother had imparted to him years before.

Player arrived at the 1959 Open Championship ten days early to practice at Muirfield so he could be familiar with every possible situation he might find himself in during the tournament. Prior to the start of the tournament, John Jacobs told Gary, "You have the game to win this tournament. You can get in there and win if you just make yourself realize that." Those words were eerily similar to his father's "it's what's inside of you that matters" speech.

Player's calculated preparation and positive mind-set ultimately helped him accomplish the first of those four goals, claiming the 1959 Open Championship.

Two years after that Open win, Player arrived at the Masters Tournament, much like the rest of the field, as a sidebar to Arnold Palmer. Palmer, the defending champion, was off to a torrid start in 1961, winning three of the first eight tournaments. After three rounds, however, it was Player who held a four-stroke advantage over Palmer, but disaster struck, as it often does on the back nine during the final round at Augusta National, as Player made bogey on holes ten and fifteen and double bogey on hole thirteen. His disciplined nature allowed him to fight off the stretch of hard times and finish with a 2-over-par 74—just enough to claim the green jacket by a stroke.

The summer of 1962 was as low a point as Player had encountered in his professional career heading into the PGA Championship. He was fifteen months removed from his last victory, and he had even confided in a friend of his desires to "give it all up" and return to South Africa forever. Echoes of his brother's lesson about not running from his problems obviously stayed with Gary as he decided to focus on the tournament at hand and leave the decision about walking away to another day.

It was then, as Player began to concentrate on his game, that he says one of the most unexplainable feelings came over him. As he looked out across Aronimink's lush fairways, beautiful greens, and

refreshing trees, he felt relaxed and invigorated. Player decided then that he was not washed up at age twenty-four, and he backed it up by winning the PGA Championship.

That victory completely changed Player's outlook and restored his confidence. Thoughts of a possible retirement turned into thoughts of completing the Grand Slam. His sights were clearly set on winning the U.S. Open, the final leg of the Grand Slam.

That happened in 1965, when most players—and patrons, for that matter—walked past the oversize leaderboard at Bellerive Country Club, where the names of previous winners were emblazoned in bright gold, and saw reigning champ Ken Venturi's name atop the list.

The only person who saw it differently was Gary Player. His eyes saw this: 1965—Gary Player. That vision remained with him every day of the tournament right up to his final-round tee time, when he took a final glance at the leaderboard and, not to his surprise, continued to see his name atop the list of champions. His studies of Norman Vincent Peale's *The Power of Positive Thinking* had solidified the outcome in his mind.

Player tied Nagle at the end of regulation and would face him in an eighteen-hole playoff, where Player's strength of mind once again proved the difference. During the playoff, the pressure got to Nagle as his tee shot on number five hit a spectator on the head, knocking her unconscious and bloody to the ground. Player tried to reassure Nagle, but the damage was done. His next shot ricocheted off another woman's ankle, and Nagle was never able to seriously challenge Player for the title.

Player had won the Career Grand Slam—he would eventually win 163 titles worldwide in his Hall of

"If your talents are mental, you are not at a disadvantage against the physically talented person. You can plan and prepare better than he can, you can outthink him during the contest, and you can manage your game better."

—Gary Player from
The Golfer's Guide to the Meaning of Life

Fame career—and the real fruits of the victory were about to come. Holding true to a conversation he had years earlier with the USGA's Joe Dey, Player donated his winnings to charity—a portion went to cancer research in memory of his mother, and the

rest went to promote junior golf because, as Player said, "I'm a foreigner here. The American people have treated me so well that I want to give something back."

Proving once again that life certainly doesn't owe anyone anything, but sometimes it's willing to give it away if you are ready to take it.

BUFFALO BILL*

Golf's "Big Three" quite arguably could have been golf's "Fab Four."

Jack Nicklaus, Arnold Palmer, and Gary Player all had impressive nicknames—The Golden Bear, The King, and The Black Knight—to go with their impressive golf resumes. But it was Billy Casper, the quiet, even-tempered man who couldn't get a nickname to stick, who outplayed them all in the late 1960s.

Between 1964 and 1970, Casper won twenty-seven PGA Tour events, two more than Nicklaus (twenty-five) and a full six better than Palmer (fifteen) and Player (six)—*combined!*

---

*Author's Note: This story was written by golf historian Mark Cubbedge, manager of Collections and Research for the World Golf Hall of Fame.

Casper's fifty-one career victories rank him seventh all-time in Tour history. That number puts him among names like Snead, Nicklaus, Hogan, Palmer, Woods, and Nelson as the only golfers who have broken the half century mark in Tour victories. It also has him looking in the rearview mirror at names like Hagen, Sarazen, Trevino, Player, and Floyd.

Yet it is Casper's name many struggle to produce when listing the Tour's winningest golfers. Indeed, Casper's golfing career is the greatest with which the general golfing public is not familiar.

Thankfully the same is not true of those who competed alongside Casper on a regular basis.

"Billy has the greatest pair of hands God ever gave a human being," Johnny Miller once said.

Whether it was his trademark fade with the driver—a low liner that the late pro Bo Wininger said bounced like a gorilla on the run (the nickname "The Gorilla" only lasted a short time on Tour)—his pin-high approaches, or his deadly putting, Casper regularly performed with brilliant touch and feel, a point that is underscored by the fact that Casper won five Vardon Awards during his career for lowest scoring average during a season.

Amazingly, Casper, a winner of three major championships (1959 and 1966 U.S. Opens and 1970 Masters Tournament) and a member of the World Golf Hall of Fame, garnered only a fraction of the headlines as The Big Three. Yet it was Palmer who once said he feared Casper more than any other player.

Perhaps that was in part due to what Palmer experienced firsthand at the 1966 U.S. Open at San Francisco's famed Olympic Club. Palmer, leading Casper by seven strokes with nine holes to play in the championship, was gunning for Ben Hogan's Open scoring record of 276 set in 1948. While Palmer was focused and fighting for the record, Casper, who was a few strokes ahead of Jack Nicklaus and Tony Lema and had told Palmer he wanted to finish second, went out and put together a back nine of 32 against Palmer's 39. Between holes fifteen, sixteen, and seventeen, Casper gained five strokes. At the end of regulation Palmer and Casper were tied.

During the ensuing playoff Casper shot a 35 on the front, two strokes off Palmer's pace. On the par-3 thirteenth, however, Casper would erase the deficit completely by sinking a 50-foot birdie putt. From there, momentum and his rock-solid game would propel him to a 69, four shots better than Palmer, and his second U.S. Open crown.

Undoubtedly it was Casper's prowess as a putter that garnered him the remarkably limited fame he continues to receive today. During the 1959 U.S. Open at Winged Foot, Casper only three-putted once and needed just 114 putts on the week as he won his first Major championship. Hogan once told Casper that if Casper couldn't putt he'd be buying hot dogs from him at the tenth tee. (Casper contends that the day after that comment, Hogan, making sure nobody was around, quietly asked him for a putting tip.)

Chi Chi Rodriguez had perhaps the best two lines about Casper's reputation as a putter:

"Billy Casper could make a 40-foot putt just by winking at it."

"[Casper] was the greatest putter I ever saw . . . When golf balls used to leave the factory, they prayed they would get to be putted by Billy."

Casper's ability as one of the greatest putters the game has ever seen was formed, quite literally, out of the darkness.

As a young, aspiring golfer, Casper would spend hours on the putting green of a local golf course in Southern California as the sun was setting and night was falling. A friend would strike a match and break the darkness, shedding a quick, flickering light on the cup.

Casper had a few fleeting seconds to take note of the cup's location across the green as his friend inserted the match into the ground behind the hole. With the mental picture of exactly where he had seen the light engrained in his mind, Casper would address his ball and send it on its way toward the point he had burned in his mind.

"Play every shot so that the next one will be the easiest that you can give yourself."
—Billy Casper

On more than a few occasions, his stroke was followed by several seconds of silence before another match was lit so his friend could look for the ball. "It's in," his friend would exclaim. To which Casper responded: "Man, you don't have to see them. You feel them in."

Casper says putting in the dark is the best thing he ever did for his game. He explained that during complete darkness he could sense the moisture on the grass, elevation changes, and exact distances with a keen sense that seemed to spread through the air.

"I got more out of those nights on the putting green than I ever did on the practice tee in broad daylight," he wrote in *Golf Digest* in 2005.

It's hard to argue with Casper's assessment, considering what he accomplished in his career, which is only made more impressive when you consider his Ryder Cup record. No player has appeared on more U.S. teams (eight, tied with Lanny Wadkins and Ray Floyd), played in more matches (thirty-seven), or won more points (23½) than Casper. For the record, he's also tied for first in most singles points won, most foursome points won, most four-ball points won, and most singles matches won.

Unfortunately for Casper, while at the height of his career, it was his considerable allergies that made headlines instead of his stellar play. Consider the article *Time* magazine wrote on Sept. 9, 1966:

How much does a hippopotamus hamburger cost?

Who cares?

Except maybe Billy Casper, who figures that the wilder the chow the better his golf. So he occasionally tries hippo (at $2.49 a lb.), and regularly downs elk ($1.49), bear ($2.25), moose ($1.98) and buffalo ($1.89). There must be something in it. Last week Casper was the only man on this year's P.G.A. tour to have cracked $100,000 in official winnings. He thus joined the late Tony Lema, who turned the trick in 1965, Arnold Palmer, who did it in '63 and '64, and Jack Nicklaus, who did it in '63, '64 and '65.

Casper, despite all his accomplishments, gets the Rodney Dangerfield treatment. Simply no respect. Here Casper was winning golf tournaments and passing milestones, and *Time* magazine precedes his impressive run up the money list by reciting the price per pound of hippopotamus, elk, bear, moose, and buffalo meat.

The facts behind this unusual diet were severe. For years Casper had suffered from the time he ate breakfast. Unbeknown to Casper, he had seven severe allergies—wheat, citrus, eggs, peas, beans, pork, chocolate, and peanuts—many of which were breakfast foods. The result was Casper would spend

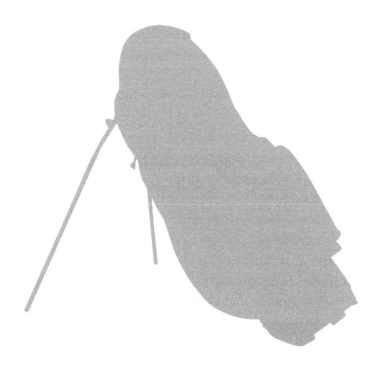

the first nine holes each round fighting off a strong desire by his body to shut down and go to sleep.

Other side effects were his nerves became edgy and, because he felt awful, he became belligerent toward his gallery—none of which helped his game.

Thankfully one doctor was finally able to diagnose Casper's allergies following a series of subcutaneous test injections. In order to prevent the buildup of allergens, Casper was put on a diet that included exotic meats. That rotation, along with a few other subtle life changes, saw Casper regain his health and enjoy some of his most productive years as a golfer.

It also saw rise to another nickname—Buffalo Bill. Casper has embraced it, incorporating the shape of a buffalo into the logo for Billy Casper Golf, his company that develops and manages golf courses for public agencies and private owners.

Casper's nickname may not be as well recognized as that of Nicklaus's Golden Bear, Palmer's King, or Player's Black Knight, but his game should be held in similar regard.

"Try to think where you want to put the ball, not where you don't want it to go."

—Billy Casper

Play Happy

Is one's path to greatness usually paved with smooth, clear lines of access, training, and success, or are the truly great ones a product of overcoming the obstacles in their path? Obstacles that would otherwise stop all others?

Such was the mental posture with which I approached the story of Nancy Lopez and her seemingly meteoric ascent to fame. I will admit that I was expecting to be regaled with stories of a childhood full of privilege and luxury. Of lazy summer days spent by the country club pool and afternoons strolling the manicured lawn called a golf course, where some latent golfing talent would reveal itself and define a golfing prodigy. Surely, it would have to be a person of deep golf heritage and a life literally growing up around the game to create so massive a star at such a young age?

In the story of Nancy Lopez and the vision and impact of her father, Domingo, I found my preconceived notions dispelled.

Nancy Lopez was not born into a life of privilege. She was born in 1957 to a Mexican-American family of modest means. Lopez learned to golf from her father, Domingo. Domingo owned a local auto repair shop in Roswell, New Mexico, the town where Nancy grew up. He believed in his heart that his daughter would one day be famous, and he and his wife, Maria, would scrimp and scrape together whatever they could to help their daughter succeed. He gave Nancy her first golf club, a sawed-off fairway wood, when she was eight years old. The family could not afford golf lessons so Domingo would be her teacher.

Experts will assert that Nancy Lopez has an unorthodox swing, and maybe they are right. Then again, didn't they say the same thing about Arnold Palmer and Lee Trevino?

Perhaps Domingo did not give his daughter a picture-perfect golf swing, but he did give her a few gems that would prove to be like a suit of armor in the heat of competition. Domingo taught his daughter to *"play happy."*

Today, it is common to see the frown-etched faces of teenage golfers who wear a scowl like a badge of honor. At what point was it determined that if you do not spend half your day on the golf course lamenting your inadequacies, then you just are not trying hard enough? Are these the virtues we are instilling in our children? Not to Domingo. He taught Nancy that attitude was as important as technical performance. That golf is a thinking-person's game and that the eventual winner is likely not the one with superior technical ability but the one who has the mental fortitude

to not tighten up under pressure. This is a powerful lesson whether one is putting for the win or trying to keep one's sanity in rush-hour traffic, with a kid to pick up at soccer practice, or trying to fit a week's worth of work into a twenty-four-hour day.

Domingo also gave his daughter the right to believe in herself. He was so convinced of her abilities that he allowed his convictions and confidence to permeate his daughter's psyche. I found this to be another powerfully simple concept: to celebrate your child's unique strengths and gifts rather than constantly harping on her weaknesses.

Nancy Lopez soon began to deliver on the promise of her talents. At twelve years old, she won the New Mexico Amateur. As a teen, she won the USGA Junior Girls Championship twice. At eighteen, she remarkably finished second in the U.S. Open. She led her high

"He was always so positive, so encouraging. He was the one who made me believe I could do anything out there. He worked hard to give me all he could. I respected him so much for that. He wanted to give me a better life."

—Nancy Lopez about her father

school golf team to two state titles. It should be mentioned that her high school golf team was otherwise composed of all men. She went on to earn a college scholarship at Tulsa (the first woman to receive a full scholarship there), and in her freshman year she was an All-American and Tulsa's Female Athlete of the Year. Lopez would turn professional at the end of her sophomore year, in 1977.

Lopez had a strong start to her first professional season, but later that year, she would lose her beloved mother after complications from surgery. As can be expected, the loss of her mother had a profound effect on such a young woman. But with the heart of a champion, she would channel her emotions with laserlike focus. She has called this time the turning point of her life and that which made her more mentally strong. In twenty-six tournaments in 1978, Lopez won nine times, including a stretch of five straight victories and a six-stroke win at the LPGA Championship. The next year, she would repeat as the Player-of-the-Year, in addition to another eight championships. Lopez would continue her solid play until she had to cut back on her playing time in 1983 due to the birth of her first child. She would end up with three girls, and in 2002 she announced that she would no longer be maintaining a full playing schedule in order to spend more time with her family.

Lopez, who was inducted into the Hall of Fame at only thirty years old, would end her full-time playing career having won a total of forty-eight championships (she would win her last tournament in 1997), and in 2000 she was recognized as one of the LPGA's Top 50 Players of All Time. Through all of this success, she continues to "play happy," infecting everyone with her warmth and charisma.

Life has a way of making us feel overwhelmed, but in the story of Nancy Lopez's life, I found inspiration from a father who chose to empower his daughter with possibilities.

CHAPTER FOUR

A FUNNY GAME

> *"Columbus went around the world in 1492. That isn't a lot of strokes when you consider the course."*
>
> —Lee Trevino

HOGAN MEETS MCCORD

When Ben Hogan was introduced to a journeyman touring professional named Gary McCord, the name didn't ring a bell with the legend. When the affable McCord explained that his humble record of no wins on the PGA Tour was likely the reason that Mr. Hogan had no idea who he was, "The Hawk" barked, "Seventeen years and no wins? You need to get a job." McCord has moved on to become one of the most popular golf broadcasters of all time.

A Tiger of a Different Color

Tiger Woods's famous tiger headcover has become something of a celebrity in its own right, often seen on television during tournaments and even starring in its own series of television commercials. As Tiger Woods is commonly credited with a killer instinct, it follows that his headcover would be a personification of not only his moniker but also of his go-for-the-throat competitive style. Alas, a closer look reveals that Mr. Tiger-Headcover may not be what the world thinks it is. In fact, it features a hand-embroidered message written in his mother's native Thai that says, "Love from Mom."

UNCOMMON CONCENTRATION

Paired with Ben Hogan at the Masters, 1948 champion Claude Harmon was the second to hit his tee shot at the par-3 twelfth hole. Hogan had already negotiated a shot to within 10 feet of the cup. Choosing a mid-iron, Harmon struck a shot that never left the flagstick, resulting in a hole-in-one. The patrons screamed wildly as the two men strode to the green and Harmon proceeded to pick his ball from the hole. However, throughout all this, Hogan remained silent, deep in his almost trancelike state of competitive concentration. After Harmon retrieved his ball, the supportive cheers respectfully went silent for Hogan's birdie attempt, which he made. With the honor on the next tee, Harmon struck his tee shot and noticed Hogan making his way over to him, clearly intending to say something and no doubt to congratulate him for his rare feat. Instead, Hogan's words were a reflection of the singular mind-set in which he insulated himself, stating that he had been waiting years to make a two on that hole!

LAPPING THE FIELD

A famous Ryder Cup match between Percy Allis and Gene Sarazen featured the assist of a woman's lap. Sarazen flew the green with his approach shot, the ball coming to rest in the lap of a woman seated next to the green. Unharmed, yet embarrassed, the woman waited patiently until told to stand up and free the ball from its blousey restraints. The woman obliged, standing up and shaking her hands and body as if shooing away a fly. The ball hopped from her garments, rolling to a perfect finish that not only stymied Allis but also provided Sarazen with an easy putt that he converted for birdie.

"You can talk to a fade, but a hook won't listen."

—Lee Trevino

"Retire to what? I'm a golfer and a fisherman. I've got no place to retire to."

—Julius Boros

PLANTING A SEED

Ironic, isn't it, that the man who planted the seed for the mega golf event known as the Ryder Cup was Samuel Ryder, a man who made his fortune selling none other than seeds!

Some Legendary Cats

A lover of golf history, two-time Masters Champion Ben Crenshaw named his various house cats Ouimet, Jones, and Hogan.

Golfer: *"You must be the worst caddie in the world."*
Caddie: *"No, sir, we couldn't 'ave a coincidence like that."*
—Henry Longhurst

"Hell, I'd putt sitting up in a coffin if I thought I could hole something."
—Gardner Dickinson

Never a Doubt

During the mid-1920s, Walter Hagen had a viselike grip on the PGA Championship, winning four in a row. However, he failed to keep such a grip on the event's trophy. After his first victory, Hagen was awarded the trophy to enjoy it for the next year as the reigning champion. Another victory meant another year in his possession, and it was sometime during this second stanza that Hagen and the trophy would part ways. Accounts have it that one night, Hagen paid a cab driver to return the trophy to his hotel, while he continued to enjoy a night on the town. It was the last that Hagen would see of it. Winning the next two PGA Championships, hardly anyone took notice that Hagen failed to present the trophy at the awards ceremony, assuming that Hagen's actions were simply a reflection of his supreme confidence and that any concern for the trophy leaving his man-tel was misplaced. Rather, it was the trophy itself that was misplaced, for after being eliminated in the 1928 PGA Championship during the semifinals, Hagen finally had to admit that he did not have the trophy and had no idea where it was, having not seen it in years. Faced with the prospect of no visual award, the PGA purchased a new trophy. Years later, the original trophy was found in a dusty old wooden crate that had been stored in Hagen's business in Florida and later shipped to Chicago. Apparently, either he forgot or it had been shipped to him and stored without his knowledge. Once found, it was put back in circulation—and now the replacement has reportedly been lost!

"Golf is a fascinating game. It has taken me nearly forty years to discover that I can't play it."
—Ted Ray

"The younger guys don't drink. They eat their bananas and drink their fruit drinks, then go to bed. It's a miserable way to live."
—Fuzzy Zoeller

IN THE SPIRIT OF THE GAME

Deep Pockets and Alligator Arms

Sam Snead had an equal reputation for being a fervent bettor on the golf course, even if in a casual round of golf, and for being very frugal in the distribution of funds for the same purposes. In other words, if you were competing against Sam Snead, you were in for a match. Remember, Sam Snead was a man who still carried a one-iron in his bag at eighty-nine years old! On one such occasion, rare though it may be, Ol' Sam finished on the losing side of a match, having been done in by a heavy allotment of handicap strokes to his opponent and an oft shaky putter in his later years. At the conclusion of his round, Snead cracked open his wallet, rubbing a twenty-dollar bill between his fingers in order to ensure he did not accidentally pull out more than the debt demanded. Snead handed over the Jackson like he was handing over his soul. Delighted, his amateur slayer pronounced, "I am going to have this framed!"

"Oh," replied Sam, "give me back the twenty. I'll write you a check."

OSCAR WORTHY

It is not unusual for the children of celebrities to feel the weight of their parents' fame. One such event took place for one of Jack Nicklaus's children, even if it was slightly off the mark. Meeting new friends at school, one excited classmate exclaimed, "He [your dad] was great in *The Shining*!"

SORRY, LUV!

Jonathan Byrd won his first PGA Tour event thanks to a particular stroke of luck. A wayward shot, destined to go out-of-bounds, slammed into the shoulder of his fiancée, bounding back into a playable position. Byrd ended up winning the tournament by one stroke.

Never Amount to Much

In 1954 the Wilson Sporting Goods Company sent Gene Sarazen to check out the game of Arnold Palmer while he was competing in the U.S. Amateur. Sarazen reported back that the young Palmer "lunged" at the ball and that the only shots he played were hooks. "I told Wilson the kid would never amount to much," reflected Sarazen.

> *"I believe if society in general conducted itself the way we golfers do, this would be a much better world."*
>
> —Ray Floyd

CHAPTER FIVE

MYSTERIOUS WAYS

GATORS' DONOVAN AND LUCK OF THE IRISH

It was a shot that never should have gone in. He was dead; in jail; out-of-the-hole. A handicap stroke in hand, wasted by circumstance and failure to capitalize, surely, victory on this critical last hole was ours and a very critical half point in our Ryder Cup–style grudge match, or so my partner and I thought. . .

The scene of our own little golf drama would play out in one of the most fabulous and inspiring golf settings in all of the world, the Old Course at Ballybunion in Ballybunion, Ireland. Gazing over Ballybunion's peaked and rolling dunes, one cannot help but wonder if this land has always been a golf course; that it was not built, but simply discovered.

Sometimes, time and space have a way of creating circumstances that seem to lift you out of the mundane, the ordinary, and let you float on a plane of the extraordinary. Such was the case on a recent golfing holiday to Ireland. The circumstances surrounding why we were there are not of particular note: eight guys who are old friends, most of whom went to school together, winding our way through the incredibly beautiful Irish countryside, ribbing each other at every opportunity, engaging in rip-your-heart-out matches and enjoying some not-so-cold pints in the glow of our far too infrequent company with each other. A celebration about where we came from, inasmuch as where we are today.

Yes, it is of note that two-time (consecutive) national collegiate basketball champion coach Billy Donovan was among our wandering nomads. Notwithstanding the worthy merits of Billy's accomplishments and the success he so richly deserves, to us he is just Billy. A kid we grew up with, graduating together in a blink of the eye, some twenty years ago. This is not to say that we are not immensely proud of him. However, for my part, I think I am prouder of the man he is, versus the success he has had. Billy is a warm and genuine person; a great father, husband, son, and friend. When you consider that he has maintained his humble humanity in a world where egos and self-indulgence are the order of the day, Billy is one of the rare cases on the national stage where you can feel secure in offering him up as a role model for your children.

"Those who succeed do so because they have made a choice to be winners—to rise above the din of doubt and reject any option except to see their dreams realized by employing the power of their passion."

—Matthew E. Adams

While the pairings were set prior to our setting out, the match in question began to build in hype the evening before. Due to my frequent travel to this beloved country, our group of eight merry men had grown to almost twice that for a raucous dinner and eclectic mix at McMunns, a peat-fire-warmed pub in dark tones, tucked away in the village of Ballybunion. Among the assembled were Jim McKenna, the Secretary of Ballybunion, Brian O'Callaghan, Ballybunion Head Professional, Stephen Mallaghan (the Mallaghans own Carton House in Dublin, site of past Irish Opens), and Jim Corr of the band The Corrs, among others. While most of the evening's discussions reflected our lot in life, and thus, focused on the activities of our children, the pitch of the evening seemed to grow in proportion to the liberal flow of Guinness. The room in which we were assembled reminded me somewhat of a cave, and it was probably a good thing as our volume and laughter must have seemed primitive at times.

Nonetheless, our dawn wake-up call the next morning arrived with particular abruptness and before we had time to finish our scones, there we were, beneficiaries of the generosity of Jim and Brian, standing on the first tee, gazing over the famous graveyard that patiently and eternally awaits the death of any tee shot sliced out of the box.

My partner was Bill Creamer, a friend for most of my life, with whom long ago I had made a pact that even if one of us developed into a scratch player, we would always play the game even, head-to-head, GHIN index be damned. On this day, we were to face the team of Donovan and John Pelphrey, the newly minted head coach of the Arkansas Razorbacks. (John's golf apparel was often emblazoned with the Razorbacks logo, which looked, to me, like a wild hog, and I was forced to wonder if the Irish people thought this giant of a man at 6 feet 7 inches was a member of a society that worships the beast. I guess in a sense, he does.)

The match unfolded as a punch-counterpunch affair with the Donovan-Pelphrey team building a three-up lead through twelve holes on the wings of Pelphrey's steadiness and the sand-trailing Donovan, whose handicap warranted a federal investigation.

On the par-5 thirteenth tee, Creamer turned to me and declared that the time to erase the deficit had arrived as the sand in the hourglass was getting thin. On my third shot, I hooked a 7-iron to the back left pin, and two putts later we shaved their lead to two up.

The fourteenth hole at Ballybunion Old is an uphill, 135-yard par 3. My partner, Creamer, won the hole with a commercial green-in-regulation and two putts. One down.

I was the first to hit at the par-3 fifteenth hole, one of the greatest par 3s in the entire world. Downhill, the green is dotted some 200 yards away, nestled between mountainous dunes and separated from the tee by rolling heather and gorse that seem to circle and stalk, waiting to devour your ball like a lion on a gazelle. The wind started to swirl, and we decided that the hole was playing more like 210 yards. I started to blindly reach down for my 5-wood when my searching hand was blocked by the hand of my curmudgeon-like Irish caddie, Sean, who whispered, "The wind is shifting, lad. Hit your tree wood and git your arse into it." On cue, the wind was now quartering hard, left to right and into our faces. I started my tee shot some 20 yards left of the pin and let the wind float the ball back to the target. The ball landed in the dead center of the green and rose up the ridge in the middle of the green to settle some 20 feet below the pin. My partner employed a similar approach and after crushing his 5-wood, he would finish a similar distance above the pin. Donovan and Pelphrey, apparently not benefiting from the cagey wisdom of Sean, both pushed their tee shots well right of the green into some devilish rough. Two pars later and Adams and Creamer had brought the match to all square.

The match moved on to the par-5 sixteenth hole. This hole is a beautiful dogleg left that is reachable in two with a well-placed drive that must be threaded between a large, protecting dune and some sadistically placed pot bunkers. As he had done all day, my gruff, cigarette-dangling caddie, Sean, pierced directly into my mind, casting aside any egotistical and unrealistic aspirations, and instructed me on a route befitting my humble game. Nonetheless, I recklessly lashed at the ball with my driver, catching the ball thin, near the bottom of the face. However, luckily, the face was square at impact, and the ball sailed off on its intended line, cleared the large dune by the slimmest of margins, and settled into what Sean referred to as "light rough" (and what I would consider deep rough even by U.S. Open standards). When we reached my ball, I was surprised to see that it was sitting up rather decently.

What transpired next was a bit of a revelation. One day earlier, from a similar lie on this hole, I nearly reached the green in two by using my 21-degree, fairway utility wood. "Hit your 8-iron," Sean sternly implored, once again contradicting my unspoken mental considerations. "No, Sean, I think I'll try my utility wood," I calmly countered. It was at this point that I realized that in relative terms, Sean clearly had as much riding on this match as I did! "It's the wrong f***ing club!" he growled through clenched teeth, and he handed me the 8-iron. Of course, Sean was once again right, and my 8-iron shot split the fairway.

Meanwhile, Pelphrey and Creamer plodded along with neither player threatening to influence the outcome of the hole. However, Donovan's efforts had a significant impact. He hit a good drive to the left of mine and somehow avoided the pot bunkers. From there, he blasted a 3-wood up the long, narrow fairway that is lined by eight-story-deep heather dunes on each side. Hit with a slight left-to-right cut that was accentuated by the left-to-right wind, his shot landed some 60 feet up the side of the steep hill.

Now, I have played this course many times, and I have never seen this prickly, gorse-shrouded monster release a victim from its grasp. Yet, as if bending fate to his partner's will, Pelphrey's refrain of "Bounce! Bounce!" seemed to coach the ball in a slow-motion descent whereby it bounced all the way down and back to the fairway, less than 20 yards from the green. My ball was sitting 150 yards from the green, and it was not lost upon me that with the stroke I had to give Donovan on this hole, he laid net one, over 100 yards closer to the target.

The pin was cut front center, just clear of a steep false front and at the bottom of a green that played like an inclined pool table. "It's uphill all the way," informed Sean. "Hit an extra club and don't be afraid to swing at it." What transpired next was my finest shot in Ireland. I laced a 6-iron to within 4 feet of the cup and felt confident that with a one-putt birdie I could at least negate Donovan's stroke advantage.

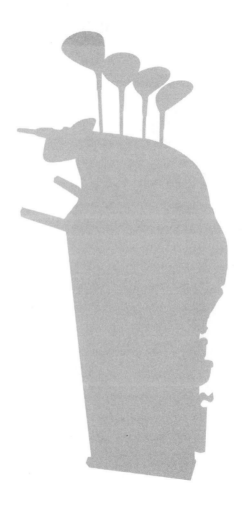

Alas, it was not to be as the great coach pinched a brilliant, low arching, high spinning wedge directly at the pin that settled some 3 feet below the hole. Two birdies later and the net eagle put Adams and Creamer back down one heading to seventeen.

The seventeenth hole is a 370-yard, par-4 dogleg left that plays downhill. Pelphrey hit one of the most massive drives I have ever seen, blasting down the right center of the fairway and disappearing from our sight behind a knoll. Donovan's drive went into the left rough behind a hill that would block him from reaching in two. My drive ended in the right rough, and I would push my approach shot into the rough on the right side of the green, pin high. Last to hit was my partner, Bill Creamer. Unfortunately, he topped his tee shot, and it plummeted down a cavern that seemed like an endless abyss. So, we all set out in different directions to negotiate our way to the green. Donovan put his third shot safely on the green, some 20 feet from the pin, sitting net two. Pelphrey's drive was hit so far that he rolled through the fairway entirely, and his ball came to rest on some ground that appeared to be under repair, yet it was not marked. Off the difficult lie, his approach missed the green. Somehow, not only did Creamer and his caddie find his ball, but he also managed to advance the ball to within 120 yards of the green. Being an experienced player, he knew that Donovan was sitting on the green in net two with a one-up lead on the seventeenth hole and that the situation was getting very, very tight. Creamer, however, rose to the occasion, punching a low 9-iron directly at the pin, where it landed, bounced once, and spun to a stop less than 2 feet from the hole. From our respective positions in the rough, both Pelphrey and I failed to get up and down and Donovan failed to convert his par/net birdie. Creamer then tapped in for his unlikely par (given how the hole began), and we headed to the final hole with the Donovan and Pelphrey side still holding a one-up margin.

The situation was now do or die. We had the honor on the tee box at the 379-yard, par-4, dogleg left, final hole that plays longer due to the uphill finish to a well-protected green. I liked hitting first because I felt that a couple of good drives in the fairway would put a little pressure on the competition. Bill Creamer hit first, and he split the fairway with a long draw. My drive finished to his right, giving both of us a clear shot at the green. Billy Donovan hit his drive left, and we lost sight of it behind a large dune just off the fairway. Once again, John Pelphrey hit a massive drive straight down the middle.

Things got interesting when we got to our balls in the fairway. Donovan's ball was not visible and required some searching to find. While this effort was under way, Creamer and I each hit our approach shots.

We both left our shots on the front fringe in very manageable positions to make par or better. Donovan finally found his ball in some ankle-deep grass. While not the deepest grass we had seen that day, it was dense, and as he slashed down with his club, the grass wrapped around the neck of the club, causing the face to shut down and the ball to rocket out well left of his intended line. It settled somewhere in a far worse position, in much heavier rough, atop a dune near the green. Pelphrey's approach also missed the green and settled in the light rough, giving Creamer and me the sense that with Donovan lost in some Druid pasture and Pelphrey missing the green, we stood a pretty good chance of winning this hole and halving the entire match. We whispered as much to one another in a conspiratorial tone as we stood by our golf balls waiting to putt our third shots toward the pin.

This is when something happened that not only had I never seen before but also that I doubt I will ever see again. Donovan found his ball nestled down into a nestlike lie among twisted heather and unforgiving gorse. Even getting a club on the ball was probably a one in ten chance at best. "Come on, buddy, get it close," encouraged Pelphrey, while Creamer and I exchanged knowing smirks. Donovan drew his club back like a sword, stabbing it down upon his entombed ball. What happened next seemed to have taken place in super slow motion. The ball jumped from its lie like a scared hare and appeared very much like it had been sculled out of its rabbit hole. At the height and speed the ball was traveling, it had no chance to touch the putting surface and would surely result in an equally difficult lie on his next shot as the ball was on a direct course to slam into the twin dune that sat on the opposite side of the green. That is when I remember hearing Pelphrey's voice barking out desperate commands. "Bounce off the hill! Bounce off the hill!" which, incredibly, the ball started to do. Somehow, its movements seemed timed to my ever increasing heart rate, and with each agonizing beat, the ball hopped from one inextricable patch of heather and gorse to another, following the commands of Pelphrey as if under power of voice remote control.

In what seemed to play out in a matter of excruciating hours that were probably only a matter of mere seconds, I suddenly heard an even more terrifying revision in Pelphrey's orders. "Get on the green, get on the green, catch the slope!" he implored.

It got worse when he started to shout, "Get in the h . . ." but he never finished the word "hole." Before he reached the final consonant, the ball slammed into the pin and disappeared into the cup.

The reality of the shot hit me in the solar plexus and drove me backward to the ground as sure as if I had been scissor kicked. While in my incapacitation, it was reported to me that Creamer collapsed first to

his knees, then into a fetal position on the ground. Meanwhile, reminiscent of Nicklaus at the 1970 Open Championship, Donovan threw his club into the air in a moment of exuberance and charged down the hill, a scene that John Pelphrey later recounted reminded him of something out of *Braveheart*. As they embraced on the green, their screams of joy and our outbursts of shock were so loud that our second foursome, some 400 yards away, said they thought the bells in the churches of Ballybunion started to ring off the echo. At the very least, every head in the clubhouse turned to find out what had happened, and the sight of two men hugging and dancing while two others lay slain for the most part spoke for itself.

For the record, Pelphrey, Creamer, and I all made par on the hole, which is not a particularly noble feat after the hole, and the match, had been decided.

We also spent a good amount of time searching for Donovan's club in the heather.

In a magic place like Ireland, I should not be surprised that something magical happened. I guess when it comes to match play competition, and more importantly, a grudge match between friends, you can't count your win before you have it and you should never underestimate the coaching skills of Arkansas's John Pelphrey or the never-say-die resolve of Billy Donovan.

Sacred Places

Winding down the coast of southwest Ireland, one must traverse the awe-inspiring beauty of the Ring of Kerry, a splendid combination of rugged coastline, quaint beaches, picturesque villages, towering hills and mountains, and prehistoric relics that tint this natural wonder like the colors in a rainbow. At the very farthest reaches of this stretch may well sit its golfing pot of gold, the Waterville Golf Links.

Like many of Ireland's great links courses, Waterville is fully capable of providing as deep a golfing experience as any course in the world. What's more, Waterville is not only beautiful but also as pure a test of golf as you can find: long in its own right, but when married with a conspiring wind, it can be a brutal examination of every part of your game. This is the course where the likes of Major champions Payne Stewart (a memorial statue of Stewart stands alongside the eighteenth green), Mark O'Meara, David Duval, Lee Janzen, and Tiger Woods would fly in prior to The Open Championship in Great Britain to become properly acquainted with the challenges and nuances of links golf. No higher compliment can be made to the caliber of a golf course's offerings.

"I think if I ran for mayor there at Waterville it would be a landslide. I don't know why they have accepted me so much, but we have a very good time there. We get into the pub and we get on the piano and I bring my harmonicas out and next thing you know it is about 4 o'clock in the morning and you go home."

—Payne Stewart

As golf often allows for the convergence of the here-and-now with more mystical realms, the twelfth hole at Waterville deserves particular note. The hole is a monster par 3, playing from a tee box atop a dune to an equally perched green dotted some 200 yards away. Interestingly, the green was originally designed to be built in the valley between these two mountains, but the Irish laborers who shaped these links simply refused to allow the green to be placed there. The reason why is that during this land's long history, the protected area between the dunes was once used as a place to celebrate Mass and conduct weddings and other religious ceremonies during a part of this country's tortured history when the same was prohibited by occupying forces. It is truly a sacred place, and you cannot help but feel reverent.

Upon completion of a recent round there, my friends and I were greeted by Noel Cronin, Waterville's secretary/manager, and invited into the clubhouse for some libation and to recount our round. Noel is typical of nearly every secretary/manager I have had the pleasure to know in Ireland. He effortlessly

represents the warm, humble hospitality so common in Ireland. Noel sat with us until after 9:00 p.m., supplying us with equal measures of Guinness and wonderful stories of Henry Cotton, Harry Bradshaw, and the many champions and characters who have helped shape the club's storied history. It was the perfect ending to a perfect day.

Driving southeast from Waterville, we set out for the town of Kinsale. As is typical of the Irish roadways in this part of the country, our journey was a paint-scraping ride along narrow country roads barely wide enough for one car, not to mention the two car widths they are often obliged to tolerate. As you never truly come to know a people until you visit their home, I felt that I had a better understanding of the Irish people's fervent grip on religion after this drive, for as a matter of practicality if nothing else, one drive down one of these roads and you learn to embrace God nearly as tightly as you are white-knuckling the door handle.

Kinsale is a lovely harbor town that is noted for its hospitality, active and varied pubs, and for its exceptional variety of gourmet food (this latter reality surprises many, but all it takes is one meal in Kinsale and the myths of bad-tasting Irish food are immediately dispelled). A few short miles outside of town sits The Old Head Golf Links, the object of our journey.

The Old Head Golf Links is a mere baby in comparison to Ireland's grand old links courses, but it is quickly making its mark on the distinguished landscape. Old Head Golf Links was built in 1997. The course sits 2.5 miles out into the Atlantic, atop a kind of octagon-shaped peninsula of land that is only accessible by driving down a narrow land-bridge that features mas-

sive caves beneath it that the sea has bored through the solid rock over the millennia. The entire area sits hundreds of feet above the violent Atlantic surf. The land is littered with ancient castle ruins (I found a stone embedded in a wall with the year 1150 carved into it in one such ruin), stone monk huts that in their starkness spoke of servitude and fervency, and the foundation of a lighthouse that dated back to medieval times. There was also an archaeologically significant, prehistoric Druid burial ground that you were forced to carry on your second or third shot into the par-5 tenth hole, lest you would be restlessly chopping your ball out of a stone-encased area of rough, gorse, and heather that had to have changed little from the days when the Druids were originally laid to rest there. Further, in what the land would surely view as more contemporary times, this was the site where the Spanish Armada came ashore and staged their attack on Kinsale/Ireland in 1601 (the Irish were soundly beaten). In different parts of the course, one can still view the steps carved into the rocks where the Spanish sailors unloaded their ships. This also was the closest point to where the *Lusitania* was struck and sunk by a German torpedo in 1915, and the place where much of the debris and bodies washed ashore. The town's graveyards are scattered with the sad graves of these innocent lost souls. Simply put, of all the golf courses I have had the pleasure to have seen around the world, I have never seen a more impressive, dramatic, or beautiful location for a golf course. The views are so scintillating that at times it is almost overwhelming. The golf course itself is a first-class, modern addition to the Irish golfing landscape and befitting of its dramatic setting.

The wonderful thing about golfing in Ireland is that every time you think your experiences have reached a crescendo, the land offers up something more to take it to a whole new level.

A Charmed Life

"Don't think this hasn't been charming."

These were the simple words that the great champion, Jack Nicklaus, said to his son Jackie as they approached their last green at the 2005 Masters Tournament.

It would be Jack's final appearance at the Masters, but his simple, heartfelt phrase was actually a bridge back in time to an emotional incident with his own father, Charlie, some thirty-five years before.

Charlie Nicklaus, an Ohio pharmacist, is remembered as being a man who embraced wholesome family values. Clearly, this was an attribute that he imparted to his son, Jack, who also is known for his famous commitment to family. In addition, Jack Nicklaus also understood the importance of what he was doing on the golf course and what it meant to his father.

"To me, my record is eighteen professional Majors, five kids, forty-six years of marriage, nineteen grandkids, and a successful business. I have other friends, I have enjoyed what I have done, and I have been able to smell the flowers along the way. Those are the things that are important to me, not the eighteen Majors. The eighteen Majors are not my life, they are part of it."

—Jack Nicklaus

"He lived for what I did. I think that was his greatest thrill and pleasure," said Nicklaus.

Some three and a half decades before Jack and Jackie would share a private moment on a very public stage, Charlie Nicklaus was dying of cancer and was being wheeled into an operating room. As he passed his family, he waved and uttered those same words, "Don't think this hasn't been charming."

Charlie Nicklaus died on February 19, 1970, at the age of fifty-six.

Jack Nicklaus used his father's death not as a source of resignation but, rather, as a source of inspiration. He had been mired in a stretch of ten Majors without winning. Nicklaus categorized his play during this time as sloppy: not putting in enough practice time or maximizing his abilities.

"I think I let him down. He would have kicked me in the rear end," admitted Nicklaus.

However, any extraneous kicks in the rear end would not be necessary. Nicklaus used his father's death as a time to rededicate himself to excellence. Nicklaus would go on to win the Masters in 1972, 1973, and 1986, the U.S. Open in 1972 and 1980, The Open Championship in 1978, and the PGA Championship in 1971, 1973, 1975, and 1980. In total, Nicklaus would win ten of his eighteen professional Majors after the death of his father.

On a spring day in Augusta in 2005, Jack Nicklaus paid tribute to his father once more as he concluded a major chapter in his own life. Fittingly, he shared this moment with his own son Jackie.

THANK YOU, DAD

I have always numbered among those who viewed Father's Day as something of a contrived holiday. Shallow on historical precedent; something fabricated for commercial reasons.

However, my jaded perspective began to thaw after the death of my father over a decade ago and I lost the chance to participate in the trite ritual. My transformation was complete the first time I received a handmade Father's Day card from my oldest son, Austin, when he was just a preschooler. Immediately, my self-righteous position was caught in the undertow of sentimentality, ushered by a tiny handprint and a misspelled message of "Dad, I luv yu."

Count me among the converted.

"In our quest to master a game that cannot be mastered, golf is foremost about self-discovery. A person is revealed to the world in a round of golf. Even more so, we are revealed to ourselves. Our character, integrity, and morality are all put to the test, and our ability to handle pressure is put to the fire. Sometimes we succeed, sometimes we fail, and if we are observant, each time we learn something new, something to keep us coming back."

—Matthew E. Adams

I realize that golf is a game that has the ability to equally appeal to males or females, but for many, it is our fathers who stand like sentries at the gates of the game, ushering us into a life-altering, and sometimes life-defining, passion.

My father instilled in me a love for the game. He taught me to appreciate the more esoteric aspects of the game, those elements that are not played out in the form of 300-yard drives or birdie putts from downtown. My father taught me that golf is a lifelong love affair. It begins with an infatuation, develops into a senseless love, and matures into a contentious, maddening, frustrating, exhilarating, fulfilling, and yet understanding kind of bond you see in an elderly couple in the park.

It is difficult to describe why the addicting game of golf is so endearing. I believe it is because the game allows us a glimpse of perfection. How often have

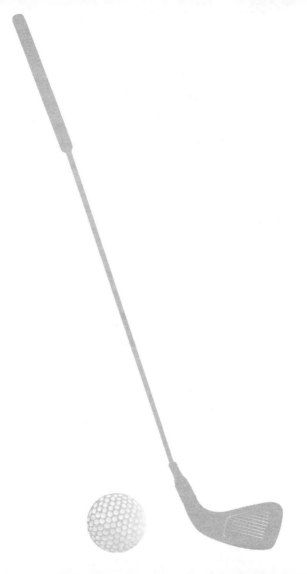

you endured a horrible round, replete with proc-
lamations of quitting the game, only to be saved
by that one miraculous shot that keeps you coming
back?

While that shot may not come with the same fre-
quency for most of us as it does for the finest golfers in the world, the game does not discriminate in
allowing us our aspirations to perfection. Why, a
first-time golfer could sink a 60-foot triple breaker or
chip in for par. Each of us has the capacity to hit a
shot with the same results as the best the game has
ever known.

What's more, golf allows us the opportunity to sometimes perform those feats on the same golf course
walked by the game's legends. What other sport
would allow such an experience?

In our quest to master a game that cannot be mastered, golf is foremost about self-discovery. A person is revealed to the world in a round of golf. Even more so, we are revealed to ourselves. Our character, integrity, and morality are all put to the test, and our ability to handle pressure is put to the fire. Sometimes we succeed, sometimes we fail, and if we are observant, each time we learn something new, something to keep us coming back.

It is for all of these reasons, and more, that golf is a game mirroring life. Golf is both a mystical journey of joy and sorrow and a physical journey of cause and effect. It is a game providing us with opportunities for wonderfully torturous choices—take a chance and achieve supreme glory or wallow in dismal failure—always with the promise of another day to try again.

To be a golfer is to be an optimist, for we all believe that our next round will be better than our last. We are always striving for more. In fact, it is the game's elusive nature that makes it all the more appealing. Ultimately, the game leaves us with more questions than answers and presents a fascinating dichotomy that keeps golf fresh and new despite its ancient origins.

My dad was right. Golf truly is like a love affair, a journey of a lifetime.

Thank you, Dad.

CHAPTER SIX

FINDING A PATHWAY TO SUCCESS

A TEXAS-SIZE ROUT

The 1967 Ryder Cup at the Champions Golf Club in Houston, Texas, was, by every measure, an embarrassing rout. The American team was without the services of Jack Nicklaus, even though he had already won two U.S. Opens, three Masters, one PGA, and one Open Championship at Muirfield, due to the strict eligibility requirements of the PGA of America. However, the team was not deficient of star power, as

"My father told me 'There will be a time and place in your career you will treasure.' I know that this was the moment he was talking about."

—Ian Woosnam, captain of the 2006 European Ryder Cup Team, on the eve of the competition (won by the Europeans)

it was anchored by Arnold Palmer and veterans Billy Casper, Julius Boros, Gene Littler, and Johnny Pott, in addition to Ryder Cup newcomers Gay Brewer, Doug Sanders, Gardner Dickinson, Al Geiberger, and Bobby Nichols.

As this Ryder Cup took place before the British field was joined by the rest of Europe (which would happen in 1979), this team of British pros was composed of seven veterans of the competition: Christy O'Connor, George Will, Neil Coles, Peter Allis, Bernard Hunt, David Thomas, and Brian Huggett, and rookies Malcolm Gregson, Hugh Boyle, and Tony Jacklin, a man who would end up being a critical part of the swing in momentum that would see the European team begin to dominate their American counterparts in today's matches.

The American Ryder Cup team did what it was expected to do. It won. Big. The final score of 23 ½ points to 8 ½ points served to underscore just how mismatched the Brits really were. The fifteen-point spread still stands as the largest margin of victory in the history of the event. While from a British perspective it would be hard to find anything redeeming in having just lost their tenth of eleven Ryder Cups since 1947 and the end of the War, it was through this depth of despair that the British golfing authorities decided to take a hard look at every aspect of their preparation. Losing Captain Dai Rees, who was also the leader of the last British team to win a decade before, recommended some dramatic changes, including adopting the larger (1.68 inches vs. 1.62) American golf ball for uniformity of performance against their counterparts and better ball control, softening up and using more water on their greens to make them more receptive and ultimately faster, playing more tournaments to get the British side better prepared, and even suggesting that the British golfers adopt a more "American style" of wedge and putter play that did not resemble their normal "pop" motion (which worked particularly well in an era when the speed and condition of greens could vary wildly from one course to the next on their Tour). While in retrospect, it may be easy to wave patriotic flags, the sad reality is that this latest trouncing in a long line of American dominance nearly ended the event altogether, as prominent voices were chirping that it had become such a one-sided affair that even the American television networks had turned down the chance to televise it, judging that the public would have little interest in an event whose outcome was predetermined before the first tee shot was even hit.

Notwithstanding the beating handed out by the Americans, the event was distinctive for a number of other reasons as well. The American squad was captained by none other than Ben Hogan. It is widely known that Ben Hogan was an intense competitor and disciplinarian, and that he had little patience (actually, none) for anyone who would dare to question his omniscient authority. One of his early decisions was to use the smaller British golf ball for this competition because it flew farther into the wind and he did not want to give up any length to the enemy. Perhaps it should not come as a surprise that an apparent, if lighthearted, challenge to Mr. Hogan would be leveled by the game's reigning king, Arnold Palmer. A private pilot, Palmer flew his own plane to the event one day after the rest of the American squad had already arrived. While he had been given permission to arrive late, Captain Hogan seemed to greet Palmer's arrival with a seething indifference. Bursting into the large locker room at the opposite end from where Hogan was sitting, Palmer called out, "Hey, Ben, is it true we are going to use the small ball?" Hogan confirmed the fact. "Well, what if I don't have any small balls?"

chided Palmer. Hogan's response was frigid: "Who said you were playing?" Palmer played nonetheless, going 5–0; however, he did sit out the morning session on the second day. When the assembled golf media quizzed Hogan as to what possible reason he had to sit Arnold Palmer, Hogan responded with the same congeniality as he had employed with Palmer himself in their earlier locker room confrontation. When asked if he could explain Palmer's absence from the morning's pairing sheet, a glaring Hogan replied, "I could, but won't."

Perhaps the height of his Hoganesque behavior took place at the pre-match banquet. British Captain Rees was the first to introduce his team, and he did so at great length, listing the individual accomplishments of each of the men in his ranks. The partisan audience applauded politely on cue. Next, Hogan strode to the podium and asked the audience to hold its applause until he was done. With that, each player on his team stood as he announced their name. He then simply said, "Ladies and gentlemen, the finest golfers in the world." The room exploded with applause that was so great that Peter Allis would later write that at that point the British team felt "ten down before a ball had been hit."

"A lot of people are afraid of winning. I was afraid I might not win."

—Arnold Palmer

Hogan ruled his team with an iron fist, instituting a 10:30 p.m. curfew and barring participation in all but the official social events. He required his squad to engage in long practice sessions and, in an apparent effort to motivate, was heard to utter, "I've never seen so many god-awful shots in my life," as he marched behind his team at the practice range.

Hogan's victorious captaincy would serve as his swan song with the event. To no one's shock, Hogan would finish his Ryder Cup career undefeated, both as a player ('47 and '51) and as a three-time captain in 1947, 1949, and 1967.

Owning All Four

They said it couldn't be done, and virtually the entire golfing public believed them. For a man to win all four Major championships in his lifetime was a feat of, well, major proportions. To win all four in succession should have been an impossibility.

Tiger Woods by now should have accustomed us to the idea of doing the undoable. He won all of them—the Masters, the U.S. Open, The Open Championship, and PGA Championship—in a one-year span covering 2000 and 2001. While it wasn't the "Grand Slam"—winning all four in one calendar year—nonetheless it was still the only time in history that a competitor won all four in succession. Sportswriters dubbed it the "Tiger Slam."

And he not only did something that was previously unbelievable but he also accomplished each in unfor-gettable fashion: For the first, the U.S. Open, he won by an incredible fifteen strokes at one of America's most important courses, Pebble Beach; at The Open Championship he won by eight at St Andrews, perhaps the most famous course in the world; at the PGA Championship he not only played the first two rounds with Jack Nicklaus, the pair's only competition playing together, but he also won in a thrilling playoff over Bob May; and to complete the Slam, he prevailed over the last nine holes at the Masters in a grinding duel with Phil Mickelson and David Duval at a time when those two opponents were among the most important competitors in the game.

Tiger himself was bowled over by what he had accomplished.

"The first two that I won probably could not have happened on two better sites. It's not too often you get to play Pebble Beach and St Andrews. Pebble

Beach is probably the greatest golf course we have over here, and St Andrews is probably the greatest course in the world.

"You never get to where you want to be. That's the beautiful thing about the game, because tomorrow can always be better."

—Tiger Woods

"And to win at Valhalla [PGA Championship] under those conditions, having to make birdie after birdie after birdie, just to hang in there, that was tough. And then to do it [at Augusta National] . . . again, one of the most historic sites in all of the world, it's pretty neat."

The story begins in 2000 at Pebble Beach with the 100th playing of the U.S. Open. Woods had yet to win the tournament. He opened with a 65, just one shot better than Angel Cabrera (who would edge Tiger Woods to win the 2007 U.S. Open at Oakmont). In the second round he posted a 69, but the average score was almost 76. Tiger would have done even better, but on the eighteenth he deposited his drive in the Pacific Ocean and went on to make double bogey. But following that mishap, his lead was still six strokes.

The third round was a huge eye-opener. With the average score standing at 77.12, only Ernie Els was able to break par. The field hit only 43 percent of the greens as the winds off the Pacific soared. But Woods, after an adventure at the third hole where he made triple bogey, was the exception. He hit twelve of a possible fourteen fairways, and though he had to battle to shoot a 1-over 71, he turned the tourna-

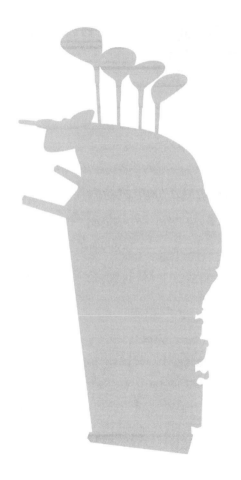

ment into a joke. His lead after three rounds was a whopping ten shots.

"I knew that if I shot even par or something close to that, I'd pick up a shot or two just because the conditions were so severe out there," Tiger said when he came off the course Saturday. Little did he know at the time that he had made the fourth round just a formality.

Sunday was a formality indeed—to everyone but Woods. He continued to bear down, and on the final nine holes he birdied 10, 12, 13, and 14. The last four holes were a coronation of his fifteen-shot victory.

"He's in another dimension," said a disbelieving Els. "I don't know what we're going to do with him."

Then it was on to The Open Championship and storied old St Andrews. By virtue of his win at Pebble Beach, Tiger had completed his mission of winning all four Majors, though not in succession. Amazingly, he had done it at age twenty-four. And he was just in his fourth year as a professional.

He would completely dominate at St Andrews, shooting 67–66–67–69, the best 72-hole score ever shot at an Open on the Old Course. And he won by eight strokes, the most in any Open since 1913.

"My dad always told me that you always have a choice. You may not like the choice, but you always have one."

—Tiger Woods

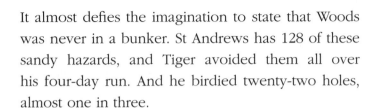

It almost defies the imagination to state that Woods was never in a bunker. St Andrews has 128 of these sandy hazards, and Tiger avoided them all over his four-day run. And he birdied twenty-two holes, almost one in three.

Woods had grabbed the lead at the end of the second round with his 66 and by the end of round three had stretched it to six. Duval posted a mild threat in round four, at one point coming within three strokes of Tiger with eleven holes to play. But Duval posted a 43 on the final nine after taking four shots in the Road Hole bunker at seventeen. Tiger breezed home the winner by eight.

Tom Watson, himself a five-time (British) Open champion, could only exclaim, "He's raised the bar to a level only he can reach."

Then it was on to the 2000 PGA Championship, held at Valhalla. This one might have been the most satisfying of all Tiger's Major championship victories because it came in a pitched, three-hole playoff battle against one of a younger Woods's heroes. Bob May was a golfing legend in Tiger's home turf of Southern California.

Tiger was in a familiar position—in the lead—going into the third round, but this time it was only a one-stroke advantage. May was one of two players who were a stroke behind, and by the fourth hole Sunday, May had surged into a two-shot lead.

Those two players staged a brilliant duel from that point until the finish. The turning point was the fifteenth, which could easily have been a three-shot swing with May looking like a near-certain three-shot leader with three holes to play.

That was the hole that saw Woods taking three shots to get to the green, facing a 12-footer for par. And needing only a little more than 4 feet for a birdie was May. But Tiger coaxed in his putt, May missed, and it was still only a one-stroke lead for May.

On seventeen, a 422-yarder, Tiger blasted his drive to lob-wedge range and made birdie to knot the score. But on eighteen, May appeared in the driver's seat again when he made an 18-footer for birdie. Woods, however, again rose to occasion, curling in a 6-footer that went into the left side of the cup.

"The putt looked scary at first," recalled Tiger. "But then I remember thinking, 'My mother could make this.' And with that thought in my mind, I got over the putt and just poured it in."

That sent the pair into a three-hole playoff, mandated for the first time ever by the PGA. Alas, there wasn't much suspense in the extra-hole affair. Woods birdied the first with a 20-foot putt while May could only par. Both men parred the second. May barely missed a 40-footer on the third hole that would have meant birdie, and Tiger blasted from a bunker to 2 feet for his par. Suddenly, Woods had his third consecutive Major. And Tiger had done it while tying May for a PGA record for lowest score in relation to par—18 under.

"This was one memorable battle," Woods said. "He matched me birdie for birdie, shot for shot. That's as good as it gets.

"This was the most exciting one, from a player's standpoint," said Woods. "The fact that you are playing at a level that is so high, and knowing that on the back nine on Sunday at a Major championship that par is not going to win any hole—that is different. Usually you can just kind of cruise in with pars and win. That wasn't going to be the case today."

That set the scene for the fourth jewel in the "Tiger Slam," the 2001 Masters. And once again, he led going into the fourth round, once again by just one

shot. This time his closest pursuer was Mickelson, although a sizzling 32 on the front nine and a birdie on the tenth hole by Duval cost Tiger his solo lead.

Standing on the par-3 sixteenth tee, Duval still had a one-shot lead. But he flew the green with his tee shot and made bogey. Woods, playing two groups behind with Mickelson, birdied the thirteenth while Duval was having his problems at sixteen. Tiger took a lead he would never relinquish, hanging on tenaciously, and dropped in a 16-foot birdie putt on the final hole to win by two strokes.

Afterward, after he had finally won the fourth Major, he talked about how much pleasure he got from going out on Sunday at the Masters and doing what was required of him to succeed at Augusta.

"The enjoyment is going out there and working for it and grinding it out and going toe-to-toe with two of the best players in the world—David and Phil—

playing really well, to go toe-to-toe with them," he said.

"That is work, but that's what it's all about. That's the fun of it. And to have that challenge, whether you win or not, that's why we play, to be able to experience that. That is the reason why I practice, to have that feeling, coming down the stretch knowing that you have to hit golf shots against the best players and somehow be able to do it."

Tiger thus had accomplished something very, very special, something that no one else had ever done. Bobby Jones won four "Majors" in 1930, but his four were the U.S. and British Opens and the U.S. and British Amateurs. Only Woods, alone among all the golfers who have played a professional golf tournament, has been able to win all four of the professional Majors in succession.

"It's hard to believe, really, because there are so many things that go into winning a Major championship," said Tiger. "For that matter, any tournament, but more so Majors, because you've got to have your game peak at the right time, and on top of that, you've got to have some luck. You've got to get some good breaks, and you've just got to have everything kind of go right.

"And to have it happen four straight times, that's awfully nice. Some of the golfing gods are looking down on me the right way."

CHAPTER SEVEN

A SIMPLE TWIST OF FATE

"There is not a single hole that can't be birdied if you just think. But there is not one that can't be double bogeyed if you ever stop thinking."

—Bobby Jones

COURAGE OVER IGNORANCE

Doing the right thing is an act of volition that should be judged without the constraints of time and the particular sentimentalities of the era in which it was enacted. Such was the case over a century ago when a young African-American golfer attempted to play in the two-year-old national championship at one of America's most storied golf courses. From any perspective, the events that unfolded were both a discomforting glimpse of the mentality in the game at that time and the nobility of the courage to overcome mass ignorance.

Shinnecock Hills, along with St. Andrews (NY), The Country Club, Newport Country Club, and The Chicago Golf Club, were the five original clubs that formed the United States Golf Association in 1894. In 1896 Shinnecock Hills was chosen as the site of the second U.S. Open. A pioneer in so many ways, from its onset Shinnecock Hills was the first club in America to allow full membership to women.

The course was built on about 80 acres of land purchased by various wealthy Southhampton, Long Island (New York), homeowners, including William Vanderbilt, Duncan Cryder, and Edward Mead. The original purchase price was reportedly $2,500, a significant sum when the transaction took place in 1891. The original architect for the twelve-hole course was Willie Davis, a Brit who emigrated to Montreal in 1890.

After Davis moved on to design Newport, emigrated Scotsman Willie Dunn Jr., whom Vanderbilt had met while on holiday in Europe and convinced to come teach golf in the United States, was hired as the club's first professional and to expand the course to eighteen holes shortly thereafter. Dunn came with significant golfing credentials and lineage. Son of the famous Willie Dunn Sr., of Musselburgh, his father once participated in a famous match featuring Jamie, Willie Sr.'s twin brother, against the formidable pairing of Allan Robertson (the first man ever to break 80 on the Old Course at St Andrews) and Old Tom Morris. As much grudge match as a competitive and betting spectacle, this was the manner in which the best golfers were determined prior to 1860 and the birth of the Open Championship at Prestwick. The match was contested over three courses, the Old Course, North Berwick and Musselburgh. It is said that Robertson and Old Tom never lost a match, and the legend handed down on this one is they came away with victory once again.

However, it is known that this chapter of the match conducted at Musselburgh went to the Dunn squad by the embarrassing margin of twelve and eleven, giving them cause for some measure of satisfaction.

Shinnecock would be tweaked several times over the years with the most significant remodeling coming in 1928 by architect William Flynn, necessitated by the planned routing of Route 27 through a number of the course's southern holes. The redesigned course, the essential layout that exists today, was opened on July 1, 1931.

But for the 1896 U.S. Open, the thirty-two entrants in the championship would play Dunn's eighteen-hole layout. Dunn himself participated, finishing in a respectable twelfth place.

Also in the field, in what had to have been shocking for the period, was a sixteen-year-old golfer named John Matthew Shippen Jr., an African American, whose father was a Presbyterian minister on the nearby Shinnecock Reservation. Entering alongside Shippen was his friend Oscar Bunn, a Shinnecock Indian who had worked on the crew that built the golf course.

"People thought I was boring. I used to just hit it in the fairway, onto the green, then hole the putt."

—Byron Nelson

Shippen, one of nine siblings of John Sr. and Eliza Shippen, moved to Southampton at ten years old, when his father accepted the position. He and Bunn started caddying at the course soon after it opened and were bit by the golf bug. Recognizing talent in the youths, Dunn took them under his wing and began to coach them. Shippen was hired as one of Dunn's assistants, where he would help give lessons to the membership, repair clubs, and join Bunn in occasionally working on the course as well. It is significant that with the appointment, Shippen would become the first African-American golf professional in the United States. However, his role was not totally shocking when one considers that in post-industrial revolution America, professionals were little more than "golf servants" to the wealthy, essentially caretakers to their enjoyment of the game versus a position of prestige (that would not come about until the time of Hagen).

A day before the tournament was scheduled to begin, several of the other professionals in the field approached Newport Country Club's Theodore Havemeyer, who was administering the tournament and was the USGA president, and threatened to withdraw if Shippen and Bunn were allowed to compete. Havemeyer would not be coerced nor threatened. He made an enlightened decision that even if every other competitor decided to walk away, then the U.S. Open would be conducted with only Shippen and Bunn in the field. Havemeyer and the other tournament officials spent a nervous night and morning waiting to see if anyone would show up for their assigned tee times. Backing down from their threat, everyone showed up and the tournament proceeded as scheduled.

In the first round, Shippen was paired with the colorful and bombastic Charles Blair MacDonald, designer of The Chicago Golf Club. The year before, MacDonald won the first U.S. Amateur, conducted at Newport Country Club. It should be noted that two prior tournaments were held that claimed to define the best amateur golfer in the country, and on both occasions MacDonald lost. Due to the fact that he was convinced that he was the best amateur golfer in the country, he could not live with these results and he fumed and complained until both events were discredited. This led the aforementioned founding clubs to form a national governing body for the sport to

administer national championships without dissent. For this reason, among others, MacDonald was one of the founding fathers for the game in the United States. His passion was nurtured during his days as a student at St Andrews University. In later years, when he began designing golf courses with Seth Raynor, he incorporated many of the Scottish design concepts he carried home with him from his undergraduate days. Perhaps his most famous course is The National Golf Links that sits next to Shinnecock. MacDonald was one of the greatest characters the game has ever known. It is said that once a member at "The National" suggested that a windmill should be added to the course. MacDonald agreed, had it built over a former water tower, then put the bill to construct the windmill in the member's locker. He was unyielding, uncompromising, a fierce competitor, and he possessed a larger-than-life ego. His singular passion for the game and powerful personality were exactly what the game needed in those delicate early years.

Shippen played a solid first round, posting a score of 78, two strokes off the lead, and tied with four oth-

ers for second place. MacDonald would shoot an 83 and was so enraged at his performance he refused to play in the second round (the competition was thirty-six holes in those days). However, it is reported that MacDonald was very impressed with the young man, Shippen, the youngest player in the field. He reportedly walked the course and kept score for him in the afternoon.

Shippen was cruising along nicely in the final round, making the turn with a legitimate shot at winning, until he reached the relatively simple thirteenth hole, a hole he had mastered many times before in casual rounds at the club. "It was a little, simple hole," was the way he described the hole in an interview with *Tuesday Magazine* many years after the tournament. Shippen knew that his drive had to be played to the right side of the fairway on this par 4 to open up the green. However, he overcompensated, and his drive landed on a sandy dirt road that ran adjacent to the hole. In the days before a sand wedge, Shippen could not extract the ball from the sandy trail, and after playing shot after shot down the road, he would eventually post a devastating score of eleven on the hole. It was a score, and a hole, that would haunt him for the rest of his life. "You know, I've wished a hundred times I could have played that little par 4 again," he would continue in the same interview. "It sure would have been something to win that day."

Shippen would end up posting a score of 81, finishing in fifth place (and winning $10). Bunn would also play respectably well, finishing in twenty-first place.

Two years later, Shippen's father would finish his tenure as pastor on the Reservation, and he moved everyone in his family back to Washington, D.C., everyone that is, except eighteen-year-old John, who decided that golf would be his life's vocation. He worked at a number of golf clubs over the years, eventually settling at the Shady Rest Golf Course in New Jersey in 1924, a position he would hold until his retirement in 1960. In the interview with *Tuesday Magazine*, Shippen wondered aloud if he had made the right decision to forgo a more formal education by going into golf full-time. "I wonder until I look out the window and see that golf course. Then I realize how much enjoyment I've gotten out of the game, and I don't wonder anymore," he concluded.

Shippen would compete in four more U.S. Opens in 1899, 1900, 1902, and 1913, with his best finish in those being a fifth place finish in 1902. His last Open, in 1913 at The Country Club, was distinctive because it was won by Francis Ouimet, who had to overcome restrictions of social status to triumph.

After 1913, the next time an African American would play in a U.S. Open would be Ted Rhodes in 1948.

John Shippen died in 1968 at the age of eighty-eight.

A COLLISION WITH FATE

Ben Hogan won ten times in 1948 and demonstrated a mastery over full post-war fields that defined his legend.

The year 1949 began in equally promising fashion as he won the Long Beach Open in a playoff and finished second the next week, after losing in a playoff, at the Arizona Open. Both the playoff victory and the loss were to his friend Jimmy Demaret.

Deciding that they needed a little time off, Ben and Valerie Hogan climbed into their black Cadillac and set off for their new Texas home. Ben Hogan was driving when a heavy fog descended like a thick blanket upon the west Texas highway. In response to the conditions, Hogan reduced his speed to a

mere crawl. While they were crossing a cement-lined bridge, a Greyhound bus that was passing a truck suddenly pulled into the Hogans' lane without any possibility of avoiding a collision. Hogan jerked his car to the right as far as he could. "Honey, he's going to hit us!" screamed Valerie Hogan seconds before the nearly 20,000-pound bus hit them head-on on the driver's side.

Ben Hogan's devotion to his loving wife has never been in question, and he demonstrated his selfless commitment to her by throwing his body across her a mere fraction of a second before the crash. Hogan's act undoubtedly saved his wife from being thrown through the windshield, and she escaped with minor injuries. Hogan likely saved his own life as well, as the force of the crash drove the steering wheel through the driver's side seat. However, Hogan's legs were still on the car's crushed left side, where the engine now stood. His legs were badly injured. It took an hour to extract the Hogans from the mangled wreckage. In total, Hogan sustained a broken collarbone, a smashed rib, a broken ankle, a double fracture of the pelvis, bladder injuries, and deep contusions to his left leg.

Hogan was rushed to an El Paso hospital, where doctors feared the legend would not live, and that if he did, he might never walk again. Hogan developed blood clots that reached his lungs. The doctors performed abdominal surgery and tied off the main vein to his leg to prevent further blood clots from reaching his heart. A second clot was discovered, and Hogan was operated on again.

Ever the fighter, Hogan would slowly recover from his devastating injuries, although it would take more than eleven months before he could make it back to a golf tournament.

As tenacious a competitor as Hogan is remembered as being, nothing he ever did with a golf club compares to his heroic determination to regain his championship form.

Hogan would return to the Tour in 1950 at the Los Angeles Open and would, remarkably, take Sam Snead into a playoff, which Snead eventually won, in his first tournament back. But Hogan would never again be as strong as he was before the accident. Hogan's legs would ache after each tournament, and he decided to concentrate his efforts on golf's Major tournaments.

"Dig it out of the ground like I did."
—Ben Hogan

Needing to soak his legs after every round and playing golf with his legs wrapped in Ace bandages, Hogan faced his greatest obstacle at the 1950 U.S. Open, which at that time required thirty-six holes of golf on the final day.

It was a mere sixteen months after his horrific accident when Hogan hit his most famous shot. He hit a perfect 1-iron on the eighteenth hole at Merion that set up a par and secured his position in a playoff the next day with Lloyd Mangrum and George Fazio. Hogan would shoot a 69 during the playoff to secure

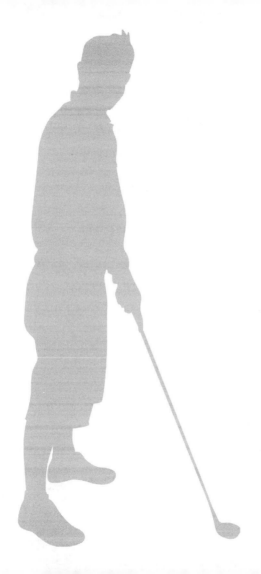

the victory. Interestingly, he would do it without the 1-iron he used the day before—the club was stolen from his bag the night before the playoff and not returned to the legend for thirty-six years.

Hogan would go on to win six Majors after the accident and a total of nine for his career.

Ben Hogan's record, particularly in Majors, is among the best the game has ever known. However, when viewed from the perspective of what he had to overcome to achieve it, it becomes clear why Hogan is one of the game's great icons.

THE HARDEST
U.S. OPEN OF ALL TIME

"Finesse has been replaced by muscle and it's due to the way our courses are set up . . . it doesn't make any difference if you keep the ball in the same country, let alone the same fairway. Sometimes you'll have better lies in the so-called rough than in the fairway."

Sound familiar? Lamenting the lost art of working the ball and courses that favor the bomber who can get home with a wedge from the grill room? Only this quote did not come from a moderate-hitting touring professional of today. The above quote is from Lee Trevino only weeks before the 1974 U.S. Open at Winged Foot's West Course. No doubt his call for more accuracy off the tee was answered in that climactic week in New York.

The 1974 U.S. Open at Winged Foot has been called many things, but foremost above them and with due merit, it has been called the hardest U.S. Open in the history of the event. However, it was also a moment of incredible convergence, a bridge from one era to the next and certainly, by every measure, a defining moment.

It helps to start with a little historic perspective. The year 1974 was deep in the throes of the Nicklaus era. He was the most dominating player of the age, and with his lethal combination of power and an exceptional mind, he was the player to beat every time he teed it up. To borrow from a similar quote by J. C. Snead: Nicklaus knew it, the competition knew it, and Nicklaus knew the competition knew it. This is not to suggest that he was without formidable competition, as players like Trevino and Johnny Miller led a mob eager to knock him off his pedestal. In addition, the game's grand and noble royalty from the previous decade still had the ability to work their magic, as evidenced by Gary Player's victory at the 1974 Masters (his second) and Arnold Palmer's resurgence. Equally as fascinating was the emergence of those who would become the next level of the game's elite, such as Tom Watson, Hale Irwin, and an amateur named Jay Haas, among others.

There are those who claim that the brutal course setup at Winged Foot was not a reaction to the birdie-fest setups of the week-by-week Tour events; rather, the genesis dated back one year earlier to the 1973 U.S. Open at Oakmont. It was there that Johnny Miller shot a final round 63 to overcome a six-shot deficit and win the tournament. Sandy Tatum, who was the chairman of the USGA's championship committee in 1974, has denied that Oakmont had any influence on his setup of Winged Foot. One thing that cannot be denied was that the course was tough, very tough.

Hale Irwin has called it the most difficult golf course he had ever seen.

In 1974 the course measured 6,961 yards (it played to 7,264 yards at the 2006 U.S. Open), which during the days of persimmon and balata was a formidable distance, indeed. What's more, in a defining moment, the fairways were sharply narrowed, the rough was very deep and unforgiving, and the sloped and undulated greens were rolling around a 12 on the Stimpmeter measure (at least).

As evidence of this latter point, an incident on the first green deserves mention. In the first round, Jack Nicklaus placed his approach shot pin high, some 30 feet to the left of the pin. Nicklaus struck his birdie putt and watched with growing concern as the putt gained speed as it approached, then rushed past the hole. The ball would keep rolling, too, eventually rolling off the green and settling approximately 35

feet from the hole, farther than from where it had begun. Nicklaus would bogey the first four holes but would end up rallying by the end of the weekend (he shot a 69 on Sunday) to finish tied for tenth place.

The first round lead would rest in the thirty-eight-year-old hands of Gary Player, who shot an even par round of 70, despite hitting only twelve greens in regulation. It was a solid round nonetheless, as the scoring average of the field was a 78 and only twenty-three players shot less than 75.

The grumbling that could be heard through the competitors' clenched teeth made the media sense a storm was brewing and demanded to know of Tatum, "Is the USGA trying to embarrass the best players in the world?" Tatum replied succinctly, "No, we are trying to identify them."

As great courses tend to produce great champions, the leaders at the end of the second day made for a star-studded leaderboard. Player shared the lead with Palmer (whose last Major win had come ten years prior), Raymond Floyd, and the journeyman, twenty-nine-year-old Irwin.

After the third round the leaderboard was equally as intriguing as a winless twenty-four-year-old named Tom Watson, who had shot a 69, held a one-stroke lead over Irwin and two shots over Arnold Palmer.

If Watson's third round foretold of the greatness that was yet to come, a final-round score of 79 would ensure that his breakthrough victory would not be at the U.S. Open (he would win two weeks later at the Western Open). Following the round, while consoling himself with a beverage in the clubhouse, Watson was approached by a man who was impressed with the young golfer's poise and talent. The older man told Watson that he liked the way Watson handled himself and that, "If you ever need any help with your game, give me a call." The man was Byron Nelson. From there a friendship flourished that helped define Watson as a Major champion and as a man.

"They don't give out the winner's check on Thursday, they give it out on Sunday. So to me it's trying to get myself prepped for that sprint to the finish on Sunday and hopefully hang in there until then."

—Hale Irwin

Palmer would miss his chance at renewed glory with a final-round 76, finishing a very respectable fifth place. Gary Player would follow his third round 77 with a 73 to finish tied for eighth place with Tom Kite (Player would win The Open Championship later that year and finished seventh in the PGA Championship).

So the championship would come down to Irwin and an obscure golfer named Forrest Fezler. Fezler trailed Watson by six shots at the beginning of the day, but he steadily made up ground as his round progressed, working himself back to 8 over par through seventeen holes and within striking distance. Meanwhile, Irwin was cruising at 5 over par with nine holes to go, only to lose two more strokes to par over the next seven holes and cut his lead over Fezler to merely one stroke. The situation did not get better for Irwin when his drive at the 444-yard, seventeenth hole landed in the impossible left rough, taking away the option to go for the green from the mangled grass. Irwin could advance the ball only 100 yards, leaving him 100 yards to the green. Meanwhile, Fezler, who had driven his tee shot into the left rough on the eighteenth hole, could do no better than make bogey, finish at 9 over par, and give Irwin a two-shot cushion. A two-shot lead may be comfortable at any other event, but not here, not at the U.S. Open at Winged Foot. Back at seventeen, Irwin hit his third shot 10 feet from the pin and sunk the ensuing putt to secure an unlikely par and demonstrate his own steely-eyed determination. Irwin played the eighteenth hole brilliantly. His drive safely found the fairway, and a laserlike 2-iron that Watson called the most pure he had ever seen set up a two-putt par that secured Irwin's first of three victories in the U.S. Open.

"What's past is past and the only future to me is the first tee shot tomorrow and go from there. That's the way I've always approached it. Simplistic and boring, but that's the way it is."

—Hale Irwin

Irwin's final score was 287, 7 over par, the second-highest winning score in the last half century (tied with Merion in 1950, Oakland Hills in 1951, and Olympic in 1955). Only Brookline in 1963 had a higher winning total when Julius Boros finished at 9 over in a weather-plagued event.

MAJOR YOUTH

In the minds of most people, it wasn't supposed to happen this way. It was supposed to be Michelle Wie striding up the eighteenth fairway, the victorious teenager in a women's Major championship, or charismatic Paula Creamer. Or any one of a dozen super-talented young golfers from Korea.

But it wasn't any of those who earned the honor of the youngest person ever to win a women's Major. It was Morgan Pressel who marched resolutely to victory in the 2007 Kraft Nabisco Championship. Morgan Pressel, who was only eighteen years, ten months, and nine days old on the day she won it. Morgan Pressel, who was in her second year as a professional after graduating one year earlier from the St. Andrews School in Boca Raton, Florida; Morgan Pressel, who first qualified for the U.S. Open while just twelve years old, who finished in a tie for second in the Open as a seventeen-year-old amateur in 2005; Morgan Pressel, who had received a total of six LPGA sponsor exemptions and never finished lower than twenty-fifth in any of them.

Of course, for every dramatic victory such as Morgan's, there's usually an equally dramatic loss. This time the loser was Norway's Suzann Petterson, who led the field by three strokes with just four holes to play at the Kraft Nabisco. When Pressel completed the seventy-second hole by draining a huge, 10-foot birdie putt, she was forty-five minutes ahead of Petterson's grouping. But the world literally changed for Pressel—and for Petterson—in those forty-five minutes.

Petterson eventually would battle back and win her Major—in the very next one she played, the 2007 McDonald's LPGA Championship. But to Pressel, the Kraft Nabisco will always be the first—first Major, first professional victory overall, the time she made history by becoming the youngest LPGA Major champion.

Detractors will point out that Pressel was not in one of the latter groups, and thus did not face the normal demands of having to win under the harsh glare of the spotlight. Supporters counter that it was a hot, dry desert day in the Palm Springs area on a golf course that was very difficult, that a tournament totals up the score after all 72 holes are played, and that Morgan was disadvantaged already by her young age.

But there was a matter of five very important putts on the final nine Sunday, three of them in the 5-foot range and the finale a 10-foot twister on the last hole. Three of the putts, on hole numbers fifteen, sixteen, and seventeen, saved par. And the slider on eighteen was huge, giving her a closing birdie and a final score of 3 under par.

Along the way, she threw in a 40-foot bomb at hole twelve, a birdie that really got her round rolling. After all, she didn't make a bogey in the last twenty-four holes.

"Those were clutch putts I made," she said in wonderment afterward. "[Number] fifteen, I missed the green, got up from the bunker, made 5-footer for par. [Number] sixteen, I hit a good shot, but it just came down the false front and I didn't hit a great putt, had about 5 feet left for par there.

"And on seventeen I got a little carried away with my putt and had about 4 or 5 feet coming back. So I knew that those were three really big important putts. Probably more important than the putt on eighteen."

But the eighteenth hole was immensely important, no question about it. She pulled a sand wedge from her bag for her approach across the lake to a pin 108 yards away. And she placed the shot within the shadow of the flag, just 10 feet away. One more putt, one huge roller that died in the heart of the cup, and she was in the clubhouse at 3 under par.

"When I made that putt, I thought, 'That's huge,'" remembered Pressel. "I knew I really needed that putt."

Of course, she had to have a little help. Petterson was four shots ahead of the teenager after saving par on the fourteenth hole, three ahead of Se Ri Pak and Catriona Matthew. All would wilt under Mission Hills' difficult conditions down the stretch.

The meltdown for Petterson began on the fifteenth, when she drove into the right rough and made bogey. It was compounded on number sixteen when she lost the drive to the right again, clipped a branch coming out, spun her third off the green, and took three putts to get it down.

Pressel had finished the eighteenth while all this was transpiring. She was three shots behind as she finished play, two shots down when Petterson began sixteen. But by the time Suzann finally finished the hole, the two were tied.

"When I went into the scorer's tent," said Pressel, "they have a television there. And I saw that she [Petterson] was in the rough on sixteen. And I kind of thought, well, it's a tough hole, you can't really miss the fairway there. And obviously I didn't know what would happen, but I knew I had a shot [at winning], I guess."

Petterson still had the advantage, however, considering she had a one-shot edge as she played seventeen, and considering that the eighteenth is a par 5, an opportunity to make birdie.

"A little help never hurts," muttered Pressel.

And then, before you could say "Major champion," it was over. Petterson fell a shot behind at the seventeenth when she missed the green with her tee shot on the par-3 hole, eventually missing an 8-foot putt and making the bogey that gave Pressel the lead. And then, needing to birdie the eighteenth to force a playoff, she missed the fairway with her drive, laid up short of the pond, wedged up to 25 feet, and missed the birdie by inches.

"Oh, my God! Oh, my God!" exclaimed a stunned Pressel.

It was only a couple of years ago that Morgan was in a similar situation, at the Women's U.S. Open at Cherry Hills. And a year ago at this Kraft Nabisco tournament, she played the final day alongside Karrie Webb, who came from seven shots off the pace to win in a playoff.

This day, though, she was more nervous waiting for play to finish than she had been playing out on the course. "You can't control what's going on," she explained. "When you're out there and when you're playing, it's a lot easier to control what you do than to wait and see what somebody else does.

"And I was waiting around there by the eighteenth, by the putting green, and it was a little hectic and a little chaotic. I decided to go over to the range where it was a little bit quieter and was getting updates from Donna Andrews, where Suzann was hitting it and whether Brittany [Lincicome] made her putt or not. There was a lot going on."

After the tumultuous victory, Morgan returned to the eighteenth green, where she took the traditional winner's leap into the adjacent pond. But despite the singular nature of competing in a golf tournament, Major victories are always a culmination of a whole community of efforts. As such, Pressel's celebration was shared by those closest to her. Joining her in her jump were her caddie, Jon Yarbrough, and her grandmother, Evelyn Krickstein. Herb Krickstein, her grandfather and the father of former tennis player Aaron Krickstein, later dipped his toes in the water.

"Aaron [Krickstein], we can go back to when I was twelve and qualified for the Open," said an overjoyed Morgan. "Aaron caddied for me that day in the qualifier, and he's a pretty good golfer himself. Obviously he's a great competitor, great tennis player, and as well as my grandfather who helped him along the way and he's helped me every step of the way."

And Pressel herself was famous now, at least in golf circles. Put behind was the heart-breaking loss at Cherry Hills when Birdie Kim holed out from the eighteenth bunker while Morgan watched in shock from the fairway.

"If I thought about it," Pressel said of the '05 Open, "I just drew on the experience that I did play so well under pressure there. Even though it was a completely different situation, I was in the last group there. And here I was coming a little bit from behind."

Most of all, though, she remembered her mother, Kathy. Kathy was the Big Ten tennis champion in 1978. When Morgan was fifteen, Kathy succumbed to the breast cancer that she had been battling for a number of years. Kathy Pressel was forty-three.

Morgan couldn't help but break into tears remembering her mother.

"I know my mother is always with me," she said. "And I'm sure she's proud of me."

CHAPTER EIGHT

THE GOLDEN AGE

*"Golf is usually played
with the outward appearance
of great dignity. It is,
nevertheless, a game of
considerable passion, either
of the explosive type or that
which burns inwardly."*

—Bobby Jones

THE UBIQUITOUS WALTER HAGEN

Imagine being third on the all-time list of Majors won and yet you played the majority of your career during an era when only three of the game's four Majors even existed? Further, consider that as impressive as that fact is, Walter Hagen is revered for raising the status of golf professionals above a simple servant class and for his starring role as golf's consummate showman.

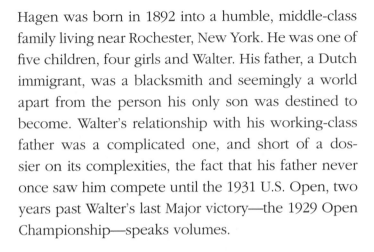

Hagen was born in 1892 into a humble, middle-class family living near Rochester, New York. He was one of five children, four girls and Walter. His father, a Dutch immigrant, was a blacksmith and seemingly a world apart from the person his only son was destined to become. Walter's relationship with his working-class father was a complicated one, and short of a dossier on its complexities, the fact that his father never once saw him compete until the 1931 U.S. Open, two years past Walter's last Major victory—the 1929 Open Championship—speaks volumes.

Hagen was one of those rare individuals who was clearly before his time. He possessed a drive, intellect, and perhaps most importantly, a vision of the emergence of the game and his starring role in it that ushered in the modern game as we know it.

Excelling in various sports as a youth, particularly baseball and golf, Hagen ultimately decided that golf would be his vehicle to stardom and the life-style that he aspired to live. Blessed with unnerving self-confidence, Hagen first came to national prominence at the 1913 U.S. Open at The Country Club in Brookline, Massachusetts. It was at this Open where a twenty-year-old amateur named Francis Ouimet beat the two top golfers in the world, Brits Harry Vardon and Ted Ray, in an eighteen-hole playoff, to mark one of the greatest upsets of all time. Finishing one stroke back was a brash twenty-one-year-old assistant professional from the Country Club of Rochester named Walter Hagen. The following year, at Midlothian in Chicago, Hagan won the first of his two U.S. Open titles in a gutsy performance over a highly experienced field. Hagen stumbled to the tee box on the first day, reeling from the effects of a less-than-fresh lobster he had consumed the evening before. Coupled with the stifling heat of a Chicago summer, the young professional hit shots that were simply ugly, following them with recovery shots that were brilliant. His up-and-down round, reflective of the way he spent the night before, not only established a new course record and the lead in the tournament but would also serve as a microcosm of the rest of his career.

"I never wanted to be a millionaire, I just wanted to live like one."
—Walter Hagen

Among his many firsts, Hagen may well have been the game's first mental coach, even if he alone was the primary beneficiary of his philosophies. Hagen was unfettered by shortcomings, mistakes, or even failure. He saw those mundane consequences as the by-products to success. Therefore he played a fearless game, for his posture was that he would take the risks necessary to succeed with a perspective that if he did not win then it did not matter if he finished second or last. Further, he anticipated adversity, even expected it. He claimed that he expected five bad shots a round (some accounts have the number at seven), so that when a poor shot would arrive, he did not see it as an omen for his round collapsing but, rather, with almost a sense of relief that he got it out of the way and only good things lay ahead. Perhaps this was the only mental posture one could have when your game was subject to so many wayward shots, but whatever the root, he played the game with a liberty that left him unshackled by fear and thus, able to think clearly when the pressure was consuming his competition. Augmenting his mental fortitude was his supreme ability to concentrate on the here-and-now, the shot at hand, despite carrying on a never-ending performance for the galleries that was another distinctive feature of this great champion.

So consummate were his abilities to recover, persevere, concentrate, and execute that in 1926 he defeated the great amateur Bobby Jones by a score of 12 and 11 during a seventy-two-hole exhibition. Hagen displayed his game in all of its classic eccentricities through the match. Shots veered wildly, both left and right, without anyone, including Hagen, knowing what direction they were likely to go. However, each time he would hit amazing recovery shots and coupled with an extraordinary short game and putting stroke, he would leave opponents in a frustrated heap. Jones was no different, commenting after the match, "When a man misses his drive, and then misses his second

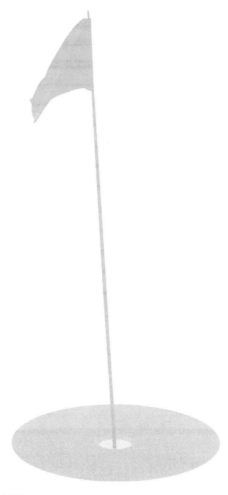

shot, and then wins the hole with a birdie, it gets my goat."

Armed with such skills, Hagen was a consummate match play competitor. Competing back in the days when the PGA Championship was match play, Hagen won twenty-two consecutive matches. While his ability to win holes was consummate, his ability to read an opponent's psyche was equally as strong. Hagen was a master at drawing opponents into his web, engaging them in discussions of national exhibition tours where their talents would earn them fame and fortune, causing his opponents to begin to concentrate on the spoils of victory before the victory had been earned. Then, with equal proficiency, Hagen would flip a mental switch, giving 100 percent concentration to the shot at hand, and deliver a crushing blow. He was known to march up to the tee box when his opponent had the honor and confidently whip a club from his bag that was either far too much or far too little than for what the shot called for. Time and again, his unsuspecting opponents would fly a green or come up woefully short, only to have Walter slip the ruse club back into his bag and proceed with the club he had always intended on using.

"You're only here for a short visit. Don't hurry,
don't worry, and be sure to smell
the flowers along the way."

—Walter Hagen

Hagen foresaw the celebrity power of an athlete who could work magic with a golf club and ball and took full advantage of his foresight by booking exhibitions

around the world and maximizing every opportunity for publicity. Hagen enjoyed life to the fullest, and he is reported to have shown up on the first tee of many an event still wearing the apparel from the night before (Hagen was an impeccable dresser and was well aware of what he was doing). He once showed up on the first tee in a top hat and tails. He was the first golfer to hire an agent, and his agent only built on "The Haig's" already larger-than-life reputation.

Hagen was equally at ease with winning Majors as he was rubbing shoulders with kings and barons of industry. As such, Hagen is rightfully credited with elevating the status of the profession by refusing to allow the star of the show, himself, to be treated with anything less than treatment befitting his status. His posture in this regard was a radical departure from the norm and was met with considerable consternation at the onset. Once, while competing at The Open Championship at Royal St. George's, Hagen was refused admittance into the clubhouse, required instead to change in the cramped offices of the golf professional's office. Instead, Hagen hired an Austro-Daimler limousine to ferry him back and forth from his posh hotel in the city, parking the eye-catching automobile in front of the clubhouse and using it to change his clothes and eat his meals. Hagen went on to win the tournament. The following year, at The Open Championship at Royal Troon, where he finished second, he was asked to come into the clubhouse for the awards ceremony. He refused the offer, countering that if he was not invited in the clubhouse during the tournament proper, he certainly would not enter now. He said that tournament officials could make the presentation in the nearby pub where he had been spending his leisure hours. Hagen's trailblazing accomplishments on behalf of golf professionals was recognized by Arnold Palmer at a testimonial dinner for Hagen, when he stated, "If not for you, Walter, this dinner tonight would be downstairs in the pro shop, not the ballroom."

"You don't have the game you played last year or last week. You only have today's game. It may be far from your best, but that's all you've got. Harden your heart and make the best of it."

—Walter Hagen

Walter Hagen was such a colorful character that it is easy to overlook his immense talent; however, he would finish his career having won the PGA Championship five times (and an amazing four in a row from 1924 to 1927), The Open Championship four times, and the U.S. Open twice, for a total of eleven Major victories. His other international titles included the French Open, Belgian Open, and the Canadian Open. He also won the Western Open, considered a Major at the time he played, five times (this is an important note because the world is willing to concede that Jones's Grand Slam included two "Majors," the U.S. Amateur and the British Amateur, while those same two events are not considered to be "Majors" today, so as a matter of equity, Hagen could be considered to have actually won sixteen Majors, placing him second on the all-time list). Hagen did compete in the Masters, known at that time as the Augusta National Invitational, however, as the Masters did not even begin until 1934, and Hagen was well past his prime. Hagen was institutional in the development of the Ryder Cup, once again seeming to grasp the event's eventual magnitude, playing a pivotal role in the first event in 1927 at Worcester Country Club (won by the Americans) and playing on the first five teams, finishing with an overall record of 7–1–1. He would serve as a non-playing captain in 1937, leading the American squad to an 8–4 victory.

As life sometimes includes ironic, if cruel, twists of fate, Hagen, a lifelong smoker, would suffer from cancer of the larynx, which would rob the great communicator of the ability to speak and ultimately take his life at the age of seventy-six on October 5, 1969.

LADY FORTUNE

Sometimes the pathway to success is lined with deep rough, unforgiving hazards, and heartless competition. It takes a firm view of the end goal, steely nerves, and, occasionally, good old-fashioned luck to hoist the champion's trophy.

Luck can be an ambiguous asset, for it has two sides. Some choose to dwell on the negative consequences of its seemingly random application, while golfers like the great Bobby Jones learned to harness its opportunities.

Such was the case with Jones's improbable march to the "Impregnable Quadrilateral," the Grand Slam in 1930. Without Jones's ability to remain patient until luck, or as he called it "Lady Fortune," turned his way, he would not be remembered today as the author of one of the greatest feats in the history of the game.

Due to the fact that Jones's conquest took place over seventy-five years ago, it is easy to discount its significance. It is only natural that we should rationalize and discount his accomplishment in measurement against the time we live in. Many today mistakenly believe that because two of Jones's Majors were amateur competitions (British Amateur and U.S. Amateur) that he did not face truly world-class competition. However, this judgment is blinded by the bias of our own age. During Jones's era, professional golf was not what it is today. Professional golfers were not the mega-media stars and multimillionaires that they are today. Being a professional in the first half of the twentieth century (at least before Hagen and others completely altered the image of a touring professional golfer) was akin to a service position. Someone to attend to support tasks such as club repair, lessons, and an occasional round of golf when duties at the country club did not prohibit. Therefore, it was not uncommon that many of the world's finest golfers chose to remain amateurs, such as Jones and Chick Evans, for example. However, it is true that Jones's amateur status meant that that he maintained his game in world-class form while playing the game about as often as today's average weekend golf enthusiast due to the demands of first his education and later, his law practice.

It is also unfair to assume that due to shorter, less manicured golf courses and the idiosyncrasies of the equipment of his era, including hickory shafts (steel shafts had been introduced to the game by this time, but Jones, who could drive the ball an impressive 250 yards, chose to continue using his trusted hickory shafts for his run to the Grand Slam), that a score of par or better in 1930 does not represent the same accomplishment in our day. To the contrary, the inherent deficiencies, irregularities, and inconsistencies of

the equipment and course conditions during his time would suggest that his scores are even more impressive than meets the eye. Can you imagine what a player of Jones's caliber would do with our modern golf equipment!

Finally, over the decades the image of Bobby Jones has grown to such a level that many believe that he rolled to each of his championships with little to no formidable competition. This too is fallacy. Jones was the greatest golfer in the world at his peak, there can be little doubt about that. However, his capturing of the Grand Slam was as much a story of vision, determination, and overcoming adversity as it was about dominance. No small measure of his success can be viewed as the unstoppable progress of inevitable fate, for his golf skills were that consummate, yet he simply would not have won the Grand Slam without some very fortuitous breaks. Innately, he possessed

the will and fortitude to use these developments to his gain.

Great examples of this exist in events that took place in The Open Championship at Royal Liverpool (Hoylake) and at the U.S. Open at Interlachen.

"I could take out of my life everything except my experiences at St Andrews and I'd still have a rich, full life."
—Bobby Jones

Two weeks prior to The Open Championship, Jones had secured the first leg of the Grand Slam by winning the British Amateur at St Andrews. As great courses tend to produce great champions, Jones's march to victory in the match play event was not without its trials. It can be argued that Jones won the British Amateur as much with his intellect as with his immense golfing talent. This point was particularly illustrated in his fourth round match against defending champion Cyril Tolley, who was Jones's opposite in almost every manner. The massive Tolley was capable of overpowering a golf course and intimidating his opponents. Jones craftily used a psychological strategy that turned Tolley's strengths into his weakness and posted a hard-fought victory by winning the eighteenth hole (with a stymie). However, while Jones left St Andrews with the coveted victory, he also left with the knowledge that he had not played to his fullest potential. If he was to continue his march to the Grand Slam, he would need to be ready for The Open.

"I was lucky to win. I've never been happier to get any cup, and I never worked so hard nor suffered so much, either."

—Bobby Jones on his 1930 British Amateur victory

The pressure that was starting to mount on Bobby Jones at this point was formidable. Perhaps in an effort to help clear his head after the British Amateur victory, Jones took a holiday in Paris with his wife, Mary, for a few days of relaxation. When he arrived at Hoylake for The Open, his game did not immediately follow. Jones held it together well enough, however, to qualify adequately and hoped that he would find his touch in the championship.

Jones bogeyed two of his first three holes to start The Open. Similar to a display that has played itself out with Tiger Woods at Major championships, part of Jones's troubles can be attributed to the fact that a photographer insisted on taking his picture while he was in his setup or backswing. Eventually, Jones steadied himself and posted a 2-under-par 70 and shared the lead with Mac Smith and Henry Cotton. Jones would post a 72 in the second round and lead the tournament by one over Fred Robson.

At this time, the final two rounds of The Open were contested as thirty-six holes on the last day. Jones's third round would begin as his first round did, with two bogies on the first three holes. Jones would end up posting a score of 74, 2 over par. Archie Compston, a 6-foot-5 Welshman, was playing a few holes behind Jones, and he was tearing it up. Compston would post bookend scores of 34 going out and coming in and would end the round with the course record and a one-shot lead on Jones as they prepared for the final eighteen holes.

It was during this final round that Jones seemed to have come back into the good graces of "Lady Fortune." Jones's tee shot on the second hole was badly sliced, and the ball sailed directly for the out-of-bounds, only before it met its doom, the ball connected soundly with the head of a marshal and rebounded wildly into a bunker on the adjacent fourteenth hole. Jones knew that fate had granted him a mulligan, and he capitalized on the opportunity by making birdie on the hole.

Jones would par the third hole to stand at even par for the round and the tournament as his closest pursuer, Compston, who had teed off almost an hour behind Jones, was sizing up a tap-in putt on the first hole for par. Compston was brimming with confidence, still riding the hot streak from his morning round. The less-than-2-foot putt that awaited Compston was nothing more than routine, and the large man carelessly stabbed at the putt to clean up his par. To his horror, his unconcerned effort left the ball perched on the edge of the cup and he was forced to settle for a bogie. The incident seemed to unnerve Compston, and his game quickly fell apart, eventually posting a score of 82.

The implosion of Compston did not translate into an automatic victory for Jones, as the great man did little to help his cause. On the short par-5 eighth hole, which Jones had birdied in each previous round, he not only failed to get up and down for birdie from just off the green but he also chunked two chip shots, missed a par-saving putt, then missed the comeback putt to post a 7, the highest score he ever shot in an Open Championship.

"One might as well attempt to describe the smoothness of the wind as to paint a clear picture of his complete swing."
—Grantland Rice about Bobby Jones

Jones's troubles were not over yet, as he posted bogies on the eleventh, thirteenth, and fifteenth holes. But on the par-5 sixteenth hole, Jones seemed to call upon the magic that defined his career. Jones hit his second shot into a bunker at the left front of the green with his ball settling into a difficult position and on a downhill lie. Jones was forced into an awkward stance with one leg in the bunker and one out. However, he executed a perfect shot, exploding the ball softly up over the bunker face and rolling it directly toward the hole for a 2-inch tap-in birdie.

Jones's final-round 75 and total of 3 over par was good enough to win The Open Championship with a two-shot victory over Leo Diegel and Mac Smith, a victory that would not have happened without some good old-fashioned luck.

Back in the United States to continue his march toward the Grand Slam, Jones's game seemed to be coming back around to a standard he expected. Perhaps being back on familiar American soil had something to do with it, but it was more likely the result of having more time to practice.

After the first round of the U.S. Open at Interlachen Country Club in suburban Minneapolis, Jones found himself one shot off the lead after posting a solid 1-under-par score of 71.

Jones began the second round in a similar fashion, needing only a par on the par-5 ninth hole to go out in 1 under par. The hole measured less than 500 yards, and it was possible to get home in two if the second shot was played over a pretty lake distinguished by beautiful lilies. Jones approached the hole with an air of confidence, as he had consistently birdied it in his practice rounds. Jones's drive was slightly pushed, and his ball settled into a barren spot near the front of the lake. Jones, still determined to get his second shot on the green, took aim over the large body of water. At the top of his backswing, Jones's peripheral vision picked up two young girls darting out of the gallery ahead of him. In a fraction of a second, his mind raced to react and the resultant swing nearly topped the ball, sending it on a knee-high trajectory that was clearly destined to land in the lake.

Once more, good fortune seemed to be smiling on Bobby Jones, for his ball skipped twice over the lake and bounded its way up to a grassy area some 90 feet short of the green. Many swore that Jones's ball was the beneficiary of a fortuitous bounce off one of the lily pads, although Jones consistently denied such assistance. What could not be denied was that a shot that clearly should have led to a bogey, or worse, now lay near the green in two. Jones would once more take advantage of the opportunity by posting a birdie on the hole and ended up finishing the round at 1 over par.

Jones would post a dominating score of 68 in the third round and hung on for a tumultuous 75 in the final round. His score was good enough for a two-stroke victory over Mac Smith and secured the third leg of the Grand Slam.

Of course, Jones would complete his quest for the Grand Slam with his victory in the U.S. Amateur at Merion. In the match play event, Jones's conquest seemed to be predetermined, and he coasted to a convincing victory. Having accomplished golf's ultimate feat and weary of the expectations to win every time he teed it up, Jones would retire at the age of twenty-eight.

Bobby Jones deserves every accolade that is bestowed upon him, but it is likely that even he would have admitted that no matter how good you are, it helps to also be lucky.

A Year of Tragedy and Triumph

Some years are so distinctive that their events become seared upon the pages of history. As though the currents of incidents building up to them could no longer be contained, ushering in a whole new era.

The Norman invasion of England in 1066, Columbus sailing to the New World in 1492, and the Declaration of Independence in 1776 are three that quickly come to mind.

Another year that still echoes through time is 1912. The sinking of the *Titanic* on April 14, 1912, while on its maiden voyage caused such shock and anguish that it will never be forgotten. Along with the mourning and anger that accompanied the massive loss of lives, it also caused a reassessment of the shipping industry's (and society's) collective hubris and

headstrong belief that adequate life rafts were a frivolous concern on an "unsinkable" ship.

In sharp contrast, 1912 would also mark the birth of three men who would redefine the world of golf, carrying it across the bridge from hickory shafts to perfectly manicured, rope-lined gardens that would serve as the world stage for the sport they dominated.

In February, Byron Nelson was born. He was followed by Sam Snead in May and Ben Hogan in August.

To say these three men made a major impact on the game would be an understatement. Collectively, they won 198 PGA Tour events and 21 Major championships. Individually, the number of tournaments they won is astounding with 82 for Snead, the all-time leader in victories, 64 for Hogan, third all-time, and 52 for Nelson, who was only recently eclipsed by Tiger Woods on the all-time list.

Each of these three men has left an indelible mark on the game.

Nelson still owns the Tour mark for the longest consecutive winning streak, with eleven, in 1945. He also won a total of eighteen events that same year. He won five Majors.

Nelson's totals would have undoubtedly been higher had he not retired to his quiet Texas farm at thirty-four years old. However, what is not widely known is that Nelson's motivation was based on more than a desire to simply become a gentleman farmer. In the second half of 1945, at the height of his prowess, Nelson suffered from piercing stomach pains and an aching back. Doctors at Minnesota's Mayo Clinic determined that the ailments were the result of stress. Nelson would play through the following season, once again winning multiple events, and would finally call it quits at the end of that year, except for competing in the Masters (even though officially retired, he would finish second in 1947 and 1950) and selected other events (in 1955, while on vacation in Europe, he was persuaded to play in the French Open, which he then won). His career would take another significant turn in the 1960s, as he served with distinction as a golf commentator for ABC Sports at a time when the young and influential medium discovered golf. In the later years of his life, he would serve as a coach to legends like Tom Watson and settle into a sort of elder statesman role, hosting a Tour event that still bears his name.

Only months before his death, Byron Nelson said, "The place I'm going someday soon will be better than any golf course or winning any championship because I'm racing for a prize that will last forever."

Byron Nelson died in 2006 at age ninety-four.

Despite the amazing parallels in their lives, Ben Hogan was a distinctively different person than Nelson. Both Hogan and Nelson were caddies at the Glen Garden Country Club. The two had little interaction at the club until the annual caddies' tournament. Nelson would beat Hogan by a stroke, the same margin of victory he had over Hogan fifteen years later at the 1942 Masters.

Where Nelson was outwardly timid and unassuming, Hogan was intense, navigating his way through life with little patience to suffer fools. He was a tireless worker, who once said, "I always outworked everybody. Work never bothered me like it bothers some people."

His hardened exterior may have found its roots in a turbulent childhood. When Hogan was only nine years old, his father, who was a blacksmith, committed suicide in the family home. But Ben Hogan was a tenacious fighter with an iron will, and this fighter's mentality would serve him well through the rigors of succeeding on the professional tours.

Hogan was so committed to achieving his dream of being a champion golfer that he actually went broke, more than once, in the pursuit of his dream. On the verge of going bust a third time, Hogan finished second at the 1938 Oakland Open, dismissing any doubts that he had what it takes to succeed. By the late 1940s Hogan found his "secret," vanquishing a recurrent hook, replacing it with a precisely controllable fade, a particularly formidable asset for the U.S. Open, which he won four times. Excluding 1949 and 1957, when he missed the U.S. Open due to injury, for the twenty years between 1940 and 1960, Hogan never finished out of the top ten.

He was a force in the rest of golf's Majors as well, winning the Masters twice, the PGA Championship twice, and The Open Championship at Carnoustie. In 1953 he won three of that year's four Majors, missing the PGA Championship due to its timing (conflicting with The Open). He is one of only five men to have won at least one of all of golf's Majors over his career.

"Reverse every natural instinct and do the opposite of what you are inclined to do, and you will probably come very close to having a perfect golf swing."
—Ben Hogan

As amazing as all of his accomplishments are, it's even more remarkable when viewed with the knowledge of what he had to go through to secure six of his nine Majors. The six came after his horrific February 2, 1949, car accident that nearly claimed his life (see page 135, "A Collision with Fate").

Ben Hogan won his first tournament, the 1938 Hershey Four Ball (with Vic Ghezzi), and he won his last tournament at the 1959 Colonial.

There is, perhaps, no one more respected in the game of golf than Ben Hogan.

Ben Hogan died in 1997 at the age of eighty-five.

Sam Snead was distinguished for his athleticism, a near perfect golf swing, incredible longevity, and good ol' country wisdom that endeared him to generations.

As the all-time leader in victories on the Tour, and with more than 140 around the globe, he could flat-out play. Self-describing his swing as "oily," Snead possessed a supple athleticism that allowed him to kick a door frame above his head well into his eighties.

"Of all the hazards, fear is the worst."
—Sam Snead

Snead taught himself how to play golf on his family's Virginia cow and chicken farm, being the youngest of five brothers.

Snead won the Masters three times, the PGA Championship three times, and The Open Championship at St Andrews in 1946. The only Major that eluded him was the U.S. Open, but not without coming very close on more than one occasion. At the 1939 U.S. Open at Spring Mill in Philadelphia, Snead needed only a par on the final hole to win the tournament. However, in an era before on-course leaderboards, Snead mistakenly thought he needed a birdie to secure the win. Instead, pressing, Snead would score a triple-bogie eight and finished tied for fifth. At the 1947 U.S. Open at the St. Louis Country Club, he missed a 2½-foot putt on the final hole to lose in a playoff to Lew Worsham. In total, he would finish second at the U.S. Open four times.

Perhaps equally as impressive as Snead's career victory totals was his longevity at the game's highest ranks. His professional career extended over fifty years.

In 1965, at the age of fifty-two, he became the oldest winner of a Tour event when he won his eighth Greater Greensboro Open. At age sixty, he finished fourth at the 1972 PGA Championship, and in 1979, at age sixty-seven, he became the oldest man ever to make the cut on the PGA Tour (he also shot his age that same weekend).

Sam Snead died on May 23, 2002, four days before his ninetieth birthday.

Some years change history and others define it; 1912, and the birth of three of golf's all-time greats, certainly did both.

CHAPTER NINE

SCALING MOUNTAINS

*"A buoyant, positive
approach to the
game is as basic as
a sound swing."*
—Tony Lema

BEN HOGAN AND THE MUNICIPAL PRO

At the age of forty-three, Hogan was still the purest ball striker on Tour. After a phenomenal 1953 season, when he had won three of that year's four Majors, the following year he had gone winless and was looking to end the streak at Olympic.

As always, his preparation was meticulous. Hogan had arrived a week early to study and practice at the recently toughened-up course. So too did an unknown golfer named Jack Fleck. Their preparation paid dividends when after the first three rounds of the tournament, Hogan was in sole possession of the lead, followed by Sam Snead and Tommy Bolt, one and two shots back respectively, and the tournament's Cinderella story, Jack Fleck, who was three shots off the lead.

The U.S. Open was still played as a thirty-six-hole final in 1955, and Hogan teed off for his final round in the early afternoon before a number of his pursuers. In an arduous final round, it appeared that Hogan had secured his fifth U.S. Open title when he posted an even par round of 70. Gene Sarazen, who was doing television commentary of the event, rushed up to Hogan as he was walking off the eighteenth green and congratulated him on his victory. Hogan said all of the right things about there still being players on the course who could catch him, although neither Sarazen nor anyone else really believed it, except, perhaps, Jack Fleck.

Fleck was on the tenth tee when Hogan finished his round, and through Fleck's first nine holes, he had cut Hogan's lead down to only one stroke. Fleck would play steady, par golf until the fourteenth hole, where a misjudged 6-iron into the green would bunker his approach and result with a bogey. Fleck was now two behind the legend with four holes to play and few, if any, believed that he could close the gap on the Lakeside Course's difficult finishing holes. Fleck would send a spark through the crowd when he would come right back with a birdie on the par-3 fifteenth hole. Pars on sixteen and seventeen set up the 337-yard, par-4 eighteenth hole to determine if he could force Hogan into a Monday playoff. Fleck chose a 3-wood for his drive on the eighteenth, but he would pull his shot and land in the left rough. From there, Fleck would choose a 7-iron, one more club than he had been playing all week, to attack the pin. He made a wise choice, as his ball would settle some 8 feet from the hole on a green that had been giving the players fits all week, including a number of four putts! Fleck continued his trancelike play, having read the break and negotiating the speed down the slippery slope perfectly, dropping the putt for birdie and securing a playoff against Hogan for the championship.

Hogan had long before changed, showered, and packed up his locker. In a somewhat surreal image that defined the man, Hogan sat very much alone in the locker room, politely acknowledging those who were congratulating him throughout the afternoon, although clearly uneasy about the assurance of the victory others were conceding. Hogan would bow his head as the roar from the eighteenth green signaled that Fleck had matched his score.

"I learn something new about the game almost every time I step on the course."

—Ben Hogan

If it appeared that the entire world had bequeathed the championship to Hogan before the first tee shot was even struck, someone had forgotten to inform Fleck of his supporting role in the drama. Both men matched pars through the first four holes, with Fleck taking a one-shot advantage on the fifth, thanks to a bogey by Hogan. It was a lead he would never relinquish, for when Hogan needed to birdie the eighteenth hole to pull into a tie, instead the great man would hook his drive into the knee-high left rough. Error was compounded by misjudgment, and Hogan would eventually post a 6 on a hole where he needed a 3.

Fleck would play a textbook fairway-green-two-putts par that would secure his victory and one of the greatest upsets the game has ever known.

While Hogan would once again contend in major championships, the victory by Fleck somehow cracked Hogan's invincibility.

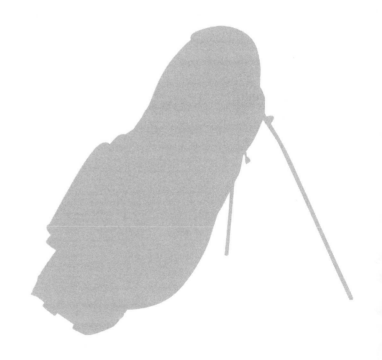

A Day in the Sun

No one ever doubted the natural talents of Tom Watson. By the time he was in his mid-twenties, he was long off the tee, laser accurate with his irons, had the ability to get up and down from anywhere, and had a bold and confident putting stroke. Such defined his physical strengths. The initial doubt, however, was his mental fortitude. A perspective that was probably unfair, as his sometimes brilliant play revealed his innate abilities that had not yet been matched by experience of tournament-hardened nerve. Probably due to the early success of a young Jack Nicklaus, critics were quick to judge a young golfer with talent if he failed to win Majors while still wet behind the ears.

Twenty-four-year-old Watson held a one-stroke lead heading into the final round of the 1974 U.S. Open at Winged Foot. Facing brutal conditions and deter-mined competition, the young golfer would falter, posting a final round score of 79. He would finish fifth, five strokes behind the winner, Hale Irwin.

Afterward, Watson sat alone in the locker room gathering his thoughts when he heard a voice. "I know how you feel, son. I've thrown away tournaments, too. If you ever want to talk about your game, call me." Watson looked up to see the legendary Byron Nelson at his side. It was an offer that Watson would take advantage of, winning his first tournament, the Western Open, soon after commencing. Just over a year later, Watson would win his first Open Championship at Carnoustie, joining the ranks of Major champions (he would go on to win five Open Championships); however, his media-placed reputation for choking when in contention dogged him. Perceived poor play while in contention at the 1975 Masters and U.S. Open did not help to eradicate the moniker.

At the 1977 Masters, that perception would change. It was a classic final round that would feature a man-to-man slugfest between Watson and the most feared man in the game at that time, Jack Nicklaus. Playing just behind Nicklaus, Watson would match the great man birdie for birdie. After making birdie on the thirteenth hole, Nicklaus would gesture with his arm to the patrons, acknowledging their wild cheering and support. Viewing this from the fairway, Watson misinterpreted the gesture as being intended for him, a pantomimed "So there!" Watson would proceed to chase down Nicklaus, eventually taking the lead with a birdie on the seventeenth hole. When the 20-foot putt dropped, the roar was so loud that Nicklaus backed away from his approach shot in the eighteenth fairway. He would later admit that Watson's birdie rattled him and caused him to change his plan of attack on the hole. Instead of firing for the center of the green, he chose to attack the pin, resulting in a shot he caught slightly heavy, which ended up in the front bunker. The ensuing bogey by Nicklaus, and par on the same hole by Watson, would give Watson his first green jacket and a two-stroke victory (he would win again in 1981 and he would finish tied for second in 1978 and 1979 and a sole second-place finish in 1984). Nicklaus shot a final round 66 to Watson's 67. It would not be the last time that Watson would stand toe to toe with Nicklaus, take his best, and persevere.

"You hear that winning breeds winning, but no, winners are bred from losing. They learn that they don't like it."

—Tom Watson

A footnote to this Masters was the lingering effect of the affair at the thirteenth hole. Watson caught up to Nicklaus outside the scoring tent and confronted him about the gesture at thirteen. Nicklaus assured Watson that the gesture was not meant for him and he meant him no ill will. Whether the incident had any lasting impact on their relationship is doubtful; however, it did serve to illustrate the fighting spirit of Tom Watson and his steely resolve to stand up to any challenge, perceived or otherwise, regardless of the source.

"I proved I could win against the big boys," Watson would say following the impressive finish.

That year's next Major stop would belong to neither Nicklaus nor Watson. Replete with its own share of drama and intrigue, the 1977 U.S. Open at the Southern Hills Country Club in Tulsa, Oklahoma, belonged to Hubert Green, who held or shared the lead in all

four rounds, finishing at 2 under par and one stroke in front of Lou Graham.

So the stage was set for a renewal of the burgeoning Nicklaus/Watson rivalry at the Turnberry Ailsa Course at the 1977 Open Championship, the first time the course would host the Championship. This was a tournament that would feature what has been called the greatest final round in Major tournament history.

The Ailsa Course at Turnberry is one of the finest layouts in the entire world. As is often the case with classic golf courses, it has a fascinating history. Used as an airfield during the Second World War, as recently as a few years ago while digging out a bunker on the second hole, an unexploded bomb was discovered buried deep underground.

In 1977, like many of the great links courses of the British Isles, it did not have an irrigation system, so if the weather was hot and dry, the course would run like a ball on an airfield runway. At its best, links courses, the quintessential test of golf, are unpredictable. When they get hard and dry, ball control can become very, very challenging, to say the least. Such was the case in July 1977. Conditions were uncharacteristically oppressive.

"No other game combines the wonder of nature with the discipline of sport in such carefully planned ways. A great golf course both frees and challenges a golfer's mind."
—Tom Watson

Prior to the start of the tournament, some thought the lack of wind and rain would actually make the course easier to play. Playing in his first Open Championship, Greg Norman speculated during the practice rounds that someone might shoot a 60 that week (Norman would miss the cut but would get revenge by winning the 1986 Open Championship at Turnberry). By the end of the week, the scoring average for the field over 72 holes would be near 10 *over* par.

Through the first two rounds, Watson and Nicklaus would post identical scores of 68 and 70, to sit one stroke off the lead, held by Roger Maltbie, after thirty-six holes. Maltbie had fired a second-round 66, after a first-round 71, to vault him into the lead. Also tied for second place were Green and Lee Trevino. Surely, it must be hard to get a good night's sleep when nursing a slim lead in front of that foursome?

The third round would belong to Watson and Nicklaus. Paired together, both played brilliant golf, match-ing each other birdie for birdie, posting matching 65s, and pulling away from the field by three strokes clear of second place, held by Ben Crenshaw, who shot a 66 in round three. Everyone anticipated that the pair would pick up right where they left off in April, and did they ever deliver!

However, the round did not start as anticipated and beguiled the drama that was to follow. Nicklaus bird-ied the second hole while Watson posted a bogey. He would then birdie the fourth hole. So, by the end of the fourth hole, Nicklaus had pulled ahead by three shots, an often insurmountable lead in the final round of a Major by any of his pursuers. Remember, Nicklaus is remembered not only for his supreme skills but also as one of the most intimidating golfers of all time. Seldom was Nicklaus the first to blink. Not only was he capable of heroics, but he also pos-sessed a supreme intellect, the ability to wait until his opponent erred, then exploiting the mistake. What's more, many doubters began to give each other wayward glances, as if to affirm that here was Watson being the Watson of their accusations; another Major opportunity spurned. But Major championships are not won by what other people think of you, they are won by what you have inside, and Watson was ready to prove, again, just how determined and convinced he was of his own mettle.

Watson would secure birdies at the fifth and seventh holes to cut Nicklaus's margin to one stroke. He would tie him with another birdie at the eighth hole, and then Watson would bogey the ninth, once again falling one behind. On the tenth hole Watson would leave his approach shot short of the putting surface, and his drive on the eleventh hole would find a bunker. On both occasions, however, he would save par. Like a snake waiting to strike, Nicklaus would tighten the noose with a 25-foot birdie on the twelfth hole to go back up by two strokes. Watson would bounce off the ropes with a birdie at the thirteenth hole to slice the margin to one, and the two would post identical pars on the fourteenth after Watson missed a 6-foot putt for birdie. On the fifteenth hole, Watson would make a birdie, putting from 60 feet off the green and slamming his ball into the flagstick, bringing the "medal-match play" to all square. The sixteenth hole also had its share of the dramatic. Watson's shot cleared a stream that cuts across the fairway but settled on the hill above it, in front of the green. For a few agonizing seconds the fate of this Championship lay in the roll of the ball from this precarious perch. If the ball were to roll even a dimple's worth back down the slope, his ball would have tumbled to the bottom of the streambed. It held, and both men would post par. The seventeenth hole is a relatively short par 5, just under 490 yards, played from an elevated tee to an elevated green. Both men hit perfect drives that split the fairway. However, Nicklaus caught his ball heavy and left his second shot finished well short of the green. Watson placed his second shot on the green in two, some 15 feet away for eagle. Nicklaus would negotiate his chip 4 feet from the hole. However, his birdie putt slid tortuously past the left side, and he would settle for par when he knew he needed more. Watson would take the lead for the first time with a two-putt birdie.

The match moved to the final tee. Watson would later admit that prior to the hole playing out, he informed his caddy that he would not be playing it safe, as he expected Nicklaus to make a birdie on the hole. (It was logical for him to feel that way as Nicklaus seemed to have a habit of making birdie on the final hole, particularly when it mattered. As in a preview of things to come, Nicklaus birdied the eighteenth hole in the first round after sinking a long, 25-foot winder.) Watson's 1-iron was played safely down the fairway, leaving a 7-iron to the green from there. Crushing into

his drive with his trademark power and fade flight path, Nicklaus's ball settled into the heather aside the fairway. Upon reaching his ball, he discovered that it had actually rolled under some gorse as well. Up first, Watson would hit one of the finest irons of his entire career, a perfectly struck 7-iron that would see the ball finish only 3 feet from the cup.

"I hit it dead flush. It was one of the best shots I ever hit. It's something I will never forget," he would later recount.

Down one stroke, under gorse and heather and facing incredible pressure, in typical Nicklausesque fashion, Nicklaus somehow found a way, tearing at the ball with his 8-iron and hitting a fabulous golf shot that finished some 40 feet from the cup.

In one of those trademark moments at The Open, the gallery closed in around the competitors, consumed with frenzy, clearly grasping that they were witnessing history in their midst. Perhaps the greatest pressure putter the game has ever known, Nicklaus proceeded to snake his 40-foot birdie putt over knolls and swales, breaks and valleys, and remarkably, into the hole for birdie. The pressure now shifted squarely onto the shoulders of Watson as his 3-foot putt must have seemed much longer at this juncture. If his tenacity at the Masters and through seventy-one holes of this Open were not enough, finally he had the chance to assert his status as a member of the club that included the greatest golfers the game has ever known. Watson's putt split the hole, securing his birdie, his triumph, and a bold new reputation.

Watson would finish with a final round 65, to Nicklaus's 66. The pair finished eleven strokes ahead of third-place finisher Hubert Green. Watson now owned his second Open title, his third Major, and with an aggregate score of 268, he beat the previous Open record, set by Arnold Palmer in 1962 at Royal Troon, by 8 strokes.

Perhaps as lasting an image from The Open as the spectacular play was when the gracious Nicklaus put his arm around the ten-years-younger Watson as they walked off the green. "You've seen my best and you have beaten it," Nicklaus would summarize.

And one of the greatest rivalries in the history of the game was in full bloom.

The Champion Within

Adversity builds character. Isn't that what they say? Perhaps it simply reveals it.

Gregory John Norman was the ultimate golfer of his era. During the time that he burst on the scene in 1983 until the ascent to the throne of a young Tiger Woods, Norman finished in the top five in each of those fifteen years. He was the number one golfer in the world seven of those fifteen years, second another three years, and third in two more.

Yet, for all his magnificence, Norman would win only two Majors, both of them (British) Open Championships. He would be in a playoff for all four but would come up short each time. In 1986 he led all four Majors at the end of the third round, but by Sunday evening, his only victory came in the United Kingdom at Turnberry.

Of all the losses that this proud Australian would suffer, however, none would match the meltdown he suffered in the 1996 Masters. That was when Norman led by a pair of strokes after the first round (when he tied the Augusta course record with 63), by four after the second round, and by a seemingly insurmountable six after the third round. Surely the fourth round would be nothing but a march to the coronation, Norman waltzing home to finally get his Masters green jacket after a career of near misses.

Except for one obstacle—a wily old veteran named Nick Faldo. The thirty-eight-year-old Faldo in 1996 was near the end of his long string of excellence—he had won thirty-five times internationally, three times was the (British) Open champion, and twice had won the Masters, both times in playoffs. And in 1996 he birdied the eighteenth hole Saturday to get into the final pairing with Norman on Sunday. Anyone else in that situation would have been awed by Norman's huge six-shot advantage. Anyone, that is, except Faldo.

"The quicker you realize that golf is not everything, the better your golf will probably be because you take your mind off of it."

—Greg Norman

The whole world might have already conceded Norman the green jacket, but not Norman himself. "I've got a lot of work to do," he said after his round Saturday evening. "I've got eighteen tough holes. And everybody's even—there is no lead. I just have to shoot a score."

Faldo conceded the obvious—he knew he had no business thinking about a victory. "It's a long way back," he said. "But, you know, anything's possible." Possible, perhaps, but no one really thought anyone else had the slightest chance.

Norman bogeyed the first hole to start Sunday, but no one took notice. He still had a five-shot lead, and his edge was still five as he played the par-3 sixth.

Faldo birdied that hole, and Norman's margin was reduced to four strokes. Well, it might not be an overwhelming victory, the patrons reasoned, but did anyone doubt that Norman would be the eventual champion? He was still playing reasonably well, and not even Faldo could predict that the Englishman might walk away Sunday evening the champion.

The eighth hole is a par 5, and Norman had birdied it three days in a row. However, he could merely par it on Sunday, and Faldo made birdie. Now the lead was trimmed to three, dangerously close with ten holes still to be played. A murmur swept through the crowd—might this really be happening? For the first time all day, there was doubt as to who the eventual winner might be. Could Greg Norman, the best golfer in the world, really blow a six-shot lead in the tournament he wanted to win above all others?

The next four holes were perhaps the four most agonizing of Norman's illustrious career. Faldo had already shown that he wasn't about to go away, regardless of the size of his disadvantage. Norman might indeed win, but he was still going to have to earn it. Faldo simply had not made any mistakes the first eight holes, and Norman had begun to show some gaps.

The ninth hole was indeed crucial. Norman's drive was fine, but his approach shot arched up onto the green and spun off. "Just a mishit," he would later say. The ball wound up back down in the valley in front of the green, leading to a bogey. Faldo, still playing mistake-free golf, knocked his ball on the green and two-putted for another steady par. Now Norman's once-imposing lead was down to merely two with plenty of golf still ahead.

Back in the clubhouse, several players crowded around the television, scarcely believing what they were witnessing. Norman had toured the front nine in 38 strokes, which in itself isn't tantamount to a defeat. However, he now was obviously out of sync. Faldo was playing brilliantly. Unless Norman could reverse the tide in a hole or two, he now was in danger of—could it be?—losing his seemingly insurmountable lead and possibly the unthinkable, the tournament.

The downslide continued at the tenth hole, however. There Faldo once again made par, two-putting from

20 feet, while Norman's troubles compounded. Norman missed the green left, chipped to 10 feet, then two-putted for bogey. His lead was down to the thinnest of margins: one. Faldo had cut five strokes off Norman's advantage in just ten holes.

And at the eleventh hole, Norman's lead would disappear completely. He three-putted from 15 feet away for a bogey, and Faldo continued to play steadily, making yet another par. They walked off the hole with the score—unbelievably it seemed—tied.

It would only require one more hole for Norman's disintegration to be complete. The twelfth hole was one more nightmarish blur. His tee-shot on this world-famous short par 3 hit the bank fronting the hole, then rolled backward into the pond. He forlornly strode to the drop zone and wedged up to the green, two-putting from 12 feet for double bogey. Ol' Reliable Faldo merely made another par. As the two walked to the thirteenth tee, Faldo had accomplished the unthinkable—he now was ahead by two strokes.

"I always wanted to be the best I could be at whatever I did. I didn't want to be the number one golfer in the world. I just wanted to be as good as I could be. I work hard, I push myself hard, and I probably even expect too much of myself."

—Greg Norman

How had Faldo done it? He hadn't performed any outlandish heroics, hadn't holed out from the fairway or shot any outrageous nine-hole scores. He hadn't made a score better than a par on only one hole. Yet he stood unshakably throughout, making up the six-stroke deficit piece by piece, stroke by stroke.

Norman should have completely collapsed by then, but to his considerable credit, he did not. He retaliated with a birdie at the par-5 thirteenth hole and came within an eyelash of making an eagle on fifteen when his third-shot chip very nearly found the bottom of the cup. He stroked in the birdie putt, making it two out of three holes that he had completed in sub-par totals.

But alas, the imperturbable Faldo didn't lose any ground during that stretch, either. He also birdied the thirteenth, reaching the green in two with a wonderful 2-iron after debating whether to hit a 5-wood. And he birdied the fifteenth hole when he chipped to 2 feet. Norman had finally righted himself, but it was too late.

Norman took his hat off to his opponent—figuratively at least—after the magnificent shot at thirteen. "He hit a great second shot, considering how many times he backed off it," Norman said. "That was the whole shooting match there."

Now playing the par-3 sixteenth still two shots behind, Norman needed a miracle—and he needed it fast. But instead he was again visited by disaster: His tee shot plopped into the water. "I just tried to hook a tee shot in there," he said, "and it hooked, all right." It proved to be a tombstone on Norman's funeral march.

In the end, though, Norman won over golf fans from around the world when he graciously congratulated Faldo. The two men warmly embraced on the eighteenth green after Faldo had completed a five-shot win, and he realized all too well the enormous difficulties that Norman had gone through.

"I just said, 'I don't know what to say, I just want to give you a hug,'" said Faldo.

Norman proceeded to the Masters interview room, where he patiently dissected the loss for all the media present. Perhaps he was still in shock, but when he entered the room, he strode in with head held high, his sense of humor still strong. "I played like [expletive]," he said, grinning broadly. "I don't know any other way to put it."

However, Norman would have his difficult time when he got back home to Jupiter, Florida. There he would spend an evening on the ocean beach, reliving the events, until he finally returned to his bed in the wee hours of the morning. He had lost Majors by playoff, lost them because an opponent holed out on him or he himself disintegrated on the seventy-second hole. But he had never, never lost one like this.

A somber Faldo said, "I hope I'm remembered for shooting 67 on the last day, and not what happened to Greg. But obviously, this will be remembered for what happened to Greg."

It was, perhaps, the most disappointing loss of Norman's stellar career. But an amazing thing happened. In the midst of his darkest hour, he endeared himself and won over a golfing public that could certainly identify with Norman's grief, his fragility, his humanity.

"I have had in excess of 7,500 letters. They are still coming in," a surprised Norman would reveal to the media at his next Tour event.

Somehow in losing, he had actually won something more. "Winning is not everything. It is how you play the game and how you accept your defeats. I think that is the most important thing," he would surmise.

Norman lost a Masters no one thought he could lose. But his composure through adversity and dignity in defeat helped define him as a champion in the most important game, the game of life.

INDEX

World Golf Hall of Fame, 47, 57

ABOUT
THE AUTHOR

Matthew E. "Matt" Adams is a twenty-five-year golf industry veteran, sports television personality, and *New York Times* best-selling author. Adams has always maintained his dual love for the game of golf and journalism. Adams started in sports radio while still in high school and went on to work at ESPN after graduating college. Adams then followed his love of the game into golf equipment manufacturing, where he designed and/or built golf clubs for Wilson, RAM, Nicklaus, Lynx, and MacGregor, among others. At the same time, Adams continued to nurture his love for writing, and in 2002 he coauthored *Chicken Soup for the Soul of America* with Jack Canfield and Mark Victor Hansen. This book benefited the New York Area Relief Fund and was a *New York Times* best seller. Since then, Adams has authored or coauthored seven books, and his books have sold over one million copies, making him one of the most successful new authors in the last five years. Adams's broadcast media work can be seen and heard all over the world on network, cable and satellite television, and radio. Adams is a member of the Club Managers Association, the Golf Writers Association of America, the International Network of Golf, and the Ancient Order of Hibernians.

Adams is also a highly sought-after corporate and event speaker. Contact him at www.FairwaysofLife.com.